THE PRINCETON REVIEW

MEDICAL SCHOOL COMPANION

Books in The Princeton Review Series

Cracking the ACT
Cracking the ACT with Sample Tests on Computer Disk
Cracking the GED
Cracking the GMAT
Cracking the GMAT with Sample Tests on Computer Disk
Cracking the GRE
Cracking the GRE with Sample Tests on Computer Disk
Cracking the GRE Psychology Subject Test
Cracking the LSAT
Cracking the LSAT with Sample Tests on Computer Disk
Cracking the SAT and PSAT
Cracking the SAT and PSAT with Sample Tests on Computer Disk
Cracking the SAT II: Biology Subject Test
Cracking the SAT II: Chemistry Subject Test
Cracking the SAT II: English Subject Tests
Cracking the SAT II: French Subject Test
Cracking the SAT II: History Subject Tests
Cracking the SAT II: Math Subject Tests
Cracking the SAT II: Physics Subject Test
Cracking the SAT II: Spanish Subject Test
Cracking the TOEFL with Audiocassette
Flowers & Silver MCAT
Flowers Annotated MCAT
Flowers Annotated MCATs with Sample Tests on Computer Disk
Flowers Annotated MCATs with Sample Tests on CD-Rom

Culturescope Grade School Edition
Culturescope High School Edition
Culturescope College Edition

SAT Math Workout
SAT Verbal Workout

Don't Be a Chump!
How to Survive Without Your Parents' Money
Speak Now!
Trashproof Resumes

Grammar Smart
Math Smart
Reading Smart
Study Smart
Word Smart: Building an Educated Vocabulary
Word Smart II: How to Build a More Educated Vocabulary
Word Smart Executive
Word Smart Genius
Writing Smart

Grammar Smart Junior
Math Smart Junior
Word Smart Junior
Writing Smart Junior

Business School Companion
Law School Companion
Medical School Companion

Student Access Guide to America's Top Internships
Student Access Guide to College Admissions
Student Access Guide to the Best Business Schools
Student Access Guide to the Best Law Schools
Student Access Guide to the Best Medical Schools
Student Access Guide to the Best 309 Colleges
Student Access Guide to Paying for College
Student Access Guide to Visiting College Campuses
Student Access Guide: The Big Book of Colleges
Student Access Guide: The Internship Bible
Student Advantage Guide to Summer
Hillel Guide to Jewish Life on Campus

Also available on cassette from Living Language

Grammar Smart
Word Smart
Word Smart II

THE PRINCETON REVIEW

MEDICAL SCHOOL COMPANION

The Ultimate Guide to Excelling in Medical School and Launching Your Career

MARY ROSS-DOLEN, M.D.
KEITH BERKOWITZ, M.D.
EYAD ALI, M.D.

Random House, Inc.
New York 1996
http://www.randomhouse.com

Princeton Review Publishing, L.L.C.
2315 Broadway, Third Floor
New York, NY 10024
e-mail: info@review.com

ISBN 0-679-76462-3

Edited by Celeste Sollod
Designed by Meher Khambata and Illeny Maaza

Manufactured in the United States of America on recycled paper.

9 8 7 6 5 4 3 2

First Edition

Acknowledgments

Nabila and Mahmoud Ali
Carl and Michelle Berkowitz
William Biles, MD, third-year resident, Geisinger Medical Center,
   Danville, PA
Mrs. Joanne Biles
Eric Dolen, MD
Dr. Andrew G. Frantz, Chairman of the Committee on Admissions,
   Columbia University College of Physicians and Surgeons
Elizabeth Higgins, MD, Assistant Professor of Internal Medicine and
   Pediatrics at Albany Medical College
Paul Clay Sorum, MD, Associate Professor of Internal Medicine and
   Pediatrics at Albany Medical College
New York Medical College

We'd also like to thank Sharyn Kolberg for her substantial editorial
   input.

Contents

Introduction

Doctors have always been well-respected in our society. As a medical student, you will find yourself in the company of some of the best and brightest students in our country. It takes hard work, perseverance, and motivation to succeed in medical school. The number of applicants is now at an all-time high; virtually every other student in your class will have undergraduate grades and MCAT scores similar to yours. How can you rise above the crowd and be at the top of your class? One of the best ways is to be prepared. *The Princeton Review Medical School Companion* will take you "inside medical school." You'll find out how to deal with the seemingly overwhelming amounts of information you'll be required to learn, what classes you are required to take, what each course will cover, and how you can best succeed in each one. The *Medical School Companion* will be your guide from the time you apply to med school to the time you take the National Boards, right on through to graduation day.

Turn on the television on any day of the week, and you will see just what society sees physicians doing in our hospitals today. But can you judge the life of a medical student by what you see on the tube? Of course not. You do not see the long study hours and arduous classwork a medical student must undergo before she even gets to the hospital setting. You do not see the sacrifices that affect not only the students, but their friends and families as well. You do not see the inner workings of medical school that go into the making of a physician.

This book will give you the insights you need to decide whether or not you really want to go to medical school, and if so, how you can make the best of the time you spend there. You will hear from students, residents, and doctors who will share their opinions of the medical schools themselves, give you tips and techniques for getting accepted into schools and residency programs, and relate stories and anecdotes that only the people who've been there can have experienced.

Come with us on the challenging, rewarding journey through medical school.

CHAPTER 1

Getting There

BEFORE YOU APPLY

How Do You Know if Medicine is For You?

Choosing a career is not easy under any circumstances, but choosing a career in medicine is especially difficult because of the sacrifices involved. It takes many years to become a practicing physician, especially if you go into any of the surgical specialties. There are voluminous amounts of material to learn. It's not always easy to adapt your personal life to the rigors of medical training. Your family life may be disrupted. The pressures of dealing with the sick and dying can be overwhelming.

However, medicine is also an extremely rewarding career. The profession is valued by society. It offers you the chance to help others, to relieve pain and suffering, and perhaps to find new methods of treating and curing disease. Medicine is an intellectually challenging and often lucrative field, and there is a broad spectrum of opportunity and career options for those who study it: there are dozens of specialties and subspecialties from which to choose. You can practice medicine in a hospital, in a clinic, in group or private practice, in a managed care system, or in any combination of these. You can go into research in such exciting and controversial fields as genetic engineering. You can even become a teacher, leading new generations of doctors.

Many people report that they knew they wanted to be doctors from the time they were very young. Other people don't decide to go into medicine until after they've been out of college for several years. There is no one path that leads people to this career. But there are certain characteristics that it is desirable to possess if you are going to succeed in the field of medicine:

- **A strong sense of commitment.** The medical student is faced with constant challenges on the way to becoming a physician. Being committed to doing your best whatever the task at hand, whether it's memorizing enzymes or treating a terminally-ill patient, is the only way to meet those challenges.

- **An interest in science and in scientific investigation.** The basics of life can be found in chemistry, biology, and physics, and the study of medicine is founded on these three disciplines. It's also based on methods of scientific investigation for evaluating symptoms, eliminating possibilities, and coming to an eventual diagnosis.

- **A love of learning.** One of the reasons a career in medicine is so exciting is that new discoveries are being made every day. Therefore, you must have the desire and ability to sort through and absorb vast amounts of information, data, research, studies, and articles— not just in medical school, but throughout your career.

- **Stamina.** Being a physician is physically, emotionally, and psychologically demanding. If your health in any of these areas is fragile it will be difficult to aid others in need. You'll need strength and energy. Many medical students and physicians participate in athletic activities both to build stamina and to release pressure.

- **Logic and organization.** Becoming a physician requires the ability to think clearly and logically, to use critical reasoning processes, and to organize study and work habits. The ability to manage your time is essential. The easiest way to get through medical school is to develop strong study habits before you get there.

Getting in

There's good news and there's bad news. The bad news is that half the people who apply do not get into medical school (on their first try). The good news is that half the people who apply *do* get into medical school. And the best news is that the rate of attrition in medical school is very low—approximately 3 percent. That means that—despite the fact that becoming a doctor requires more years of intensive education than any other professional training program—almost everyone who is accepted to medical school graduates.

What makes medical students so persistent? As one doctor told us:

> *I was an historian before I went to medical school; I have a Ph.D. in history. In graduate school, you get the sense that everyone's trying to weed you out. When I was in medical school, it was made clear from the beginning that the game was to teach us as much as possible, and to help us succeed. There really is the sense that they don't want anybody to fail. There is a strong esprit de corps, a bonding with other students. But more importantly there is the feeling that becoming a doctor is a wonderful, glorious thing, no matter what the complaints. When you enter medical school, it's constantly reinforced that what you are doing is something extremely worthwhile, not only from the individual patient's point of view, but from society's as well.*

College Preparation and Pre-Med Courses

There are three important areas to concentrate on when preparing to enter medical school:

- study habits
- basic course requirements
- extracurricular activities

Study habits

It's been estimated that medical students learn about 10,000 new vocabulary words in the first year alone. Much of the material presented to you in medical school requires pure memorization. The better your study habits before you get there, the faster you'll be able to learn and process the information.

It's most important to find the method of studying that works best for you. Some people study best alone, others prefer study groups. How you study is not as important as developing a style that works for you.

Basic course requirements

It's not necessary to choose a college, or a course of study, that specializes in premedical training. In fact, you may want to go a school where there are fewer premed students and less competition. It's not necessary to attend the most prestigious college, either. You are best off attending a college where you feel comfortable and where you're able to succeed.

You must, however, meet basic course requirements to get into medical school. For most schools, these requirements include:

Biology or Zoology	1 year with lab
Inorganic Chemistry	1 year with lab
Organic Chemistry	1 year with lab
Physics	1 year with lab
English	1 year

Some schools may also require math, computer, or humanities courses. Medical schools do not require that you major in science. In fact, studies done by the Association of American Medical Colleges show that the percentage of humanities majors (in fields such as anthropology, economics, English, and foreign languages) accepted to medical school was equal to or higher than the percentage of students who had majored in many of the scientific disciplines.

Medical schools are looking for people with varied interests and broad educational experience. As with your choice of college, your choice of major should be in an area you enjoy and in which you can do well. You're more likely to succeed in an area which is intriguing to you. Any major is acceptable as long as it leaves you time to take the required science classes.

Medical school admissions officers look at all your grades. They'll take into account your overall grade point average (GPA) as well as your science GPA. The average undergraduate GPA for 1994–95 medical school acceptances was 3.48. There are some exceptions to this standard. Admissions committees will take into consideration mitigating circumstances such as an educationally disadvantaged background or vastly improved performance in the later years of college.

Every year, more and more people decide to apply to medical school after they've been out of college for several years. In fact, in 1994–95, 5.1 percent of medical school applicants accepted were over the age of 32. Admissions officers tend to look favorably on older students, feeling that it's an advantage to have gained experience and maturity. Older applicants also often handle themselves better on interviews. However, if you've been out of college and away from the sciences for several years, medical schools want to know that you have the ability to succeed. That may mean retaking basic science courses such as biology and chemistry—which may be to your advantage if your grades in college were not very good. You will also be required to take the Medical College Admissions Test (MCAT), which all applicants are required to take. If you haven't taken a standardized test for several years, it's important that you review and prepare to get the highest score possible.

Extracurricular activities

Medical schools seek well-rounded students adept at balancing their academic and personal lives. Admissions officers are not looking for science nerds who do nothing but study and work in the lab. They want bright, motivated, disciplined individuals who have had significant involvement in college activities. These might include sports, social activities, campus politics, volunteer work, community service, research projects, Big Brother or Sister clubs, speech club, debate team, theatrical organizations, musical appreciation or performance, or any kind of special interest group. They are looking for the kind of activities that indicate leadership potential, commitment, and dedication, which means you may improve your chances of admission if you've been selected for positions such as officer of a club or captain of a sports team.

Summer and Part-time Job Experience

Qualified applicants to medical school are expected to show a genuine interest in and a commitment to the health care community. Admissions officers are looking for people who have a realistic idea of what medicine has to offer. It is to your own benefit to spend time in various health care environments to get a true idea of the hard work and long hours involved, to observe the various members of health care teams and how they function, and to interact with patients.

It is not necessary that you spend every summer doing this kind of work, nor does it matter whether you get paid or volunteer, but you should have some health-care related experience before your junior year of college. You may find work in a hospital as a volunteer, an orderly, a nurse's aid, an emergency room assistant, or a clerical worker. With proper training, it may be possible to obtain summer or part-time positions as a phlebotomist (someone who takes blood samples from patients), an EKG technician (someone who takes patients' electrocardiograms), or an emergency medical technician (someone who staffs an ambulance).

Other health care settings you may want to explore include nursing homes, rehabilitation centers, psychiatric hospitals, or clinics for the homeless. If you're interested in research, you can try for a position as a clinical laboratory assistant, or become involved in research projects at medical schools or government laboratories.

Admissions officers do take into account that some people have to work at non-medical jobs out of financial necessity. This will not hurt your chances of acceptance to medical school if all the other requirements have been met.

THE APPLICATION PROCESS

Choosing a School

In many ways, selecting a medical school is similar to selecting a college. It takes a lot of thought and study to determine which schools are appropriate for you in terms of your field of interest, your personal preferences, and your chances of acceptance.

A good way to start is to obtain literature that describes the 125 American medical schools, their specializations, faculty, workload, class size, and social life. Two important sources for this information are The Princeton Review's *Student Access Guide to The Best Medical Schools* (available in bookstores or through The Princeton Review, 2315 Broadway, New York, NY, 10024-4332, (212) 874-1754), and the Association of American Medical Colleges' *Medical School Admission Requirements* (Association of American Medical Colleges, 2450 N Street N.W., Washington, D.C., 20037-1126, (202) 828-0400).

Some of the criteria you should consider when looking at medical schools include:

- **Reputation.** You want to get into the most prestigious medical school possible. However, different schools specialize, or include specialized programs, in different areas of health care. *U.S. News & World Report*'s 1995 survey of the best graduate schools ranked the following schools at the top in various specialized areas:

Research-oriented medical schools:
   1. Harvard University
   2. Johns Hopkins University
   3. Yale University

Primary care schools:
   1. University of Washington
   2. University of California at Davis
   3. Michigan State University

AIDS research:
   1. University of California at San Francisco
   2. Harvard University
   3. Johns Hopkins University

Drug and alcohol abuse:
   1. Columbia University
   2. Yale University
   3. University of California at San Francisco

Geriatric care:
   1. Harvard University
   2. Mt. Sinai School of Medicine (N.Y.)
   3. Johns Hopkins University

Pediatrics:
1. Harvard University
2. Johns Hopkins University
3. University of Pennsylvania

Women's health:
1. Harvard University
2. University of Pennsylvania
3. University of Washington

- **Curricula.** Medical school curricula have been changing steadily over the past decade. A large number of schools still follow the traditional pattern of large, lecture-style classes, focusing on the basic sciences, for the first two years, with the second two years devoted to hands-on clinical experience.

  However, many colleges are changing that pattern, introducing clinical experience much earlier in the medical training. Some colleges are combining the two styles of learning. If you need a more structured atmosphere, a traditional education may be better for you. If you have the motivation and discipline for a more independent learning style, a school that features more small-group, problem-based learning strategies may be best for you.

- **Size.** If you attended a small college where you had a chance to get to know most of your professors and classmates personally, a jump to a large medical school may be a difficult adjustment. However, large schools usually offer more diversity in the student body and in the choice of academic and extracurricular activities. What small schools lack in diversity, they may make up in a friendly atmosphere and less competition.

- **Location.** Many students have definite preferences regarding the location of the school. You may have reasons for wanting to stay close to home, or you may want to travel to a part of the country you haven't seen before. There are, of course, other factors involved. Would you be comfortable living in a large city? In what part of the city is the school located? Are there safety concerns? Is there public transportation available? If you choose to attend a school in a rural setting, will you be happy there? Are there enough social and cultural activities available to keep you satisfied?

You must also keep residency requirements in mind when applying to medical school. Does the school accept out-of-state residents? If so, is it a significant number, or just a token few? If you have your heart set on attending a school that accepts only residents, you might consider moving to that state several months before you apply (after checking with the school to determine their residency requirements). In most cases, it isn't easy to transfer from one medical school to another; therefore, location is an important element of your decision-making process, as you'll be spending four years at the school you choose.

- **Atmosphere.** One medical school admissions officer suggests that one of the most important criteria to consider is the school's "character." How friendly—or unfriendly—are the students? Do they study in groups, or is everyone left to look out for themselves? Does the school promote a competitive atmosphere? Some students thrive in such an environment; it makes them try even harder and perform at higher levels. For others, such an atmosphere creates too much pressure and impedes the learning process. Reading about a school can give you only so much information in this area; the best means of finding out about the character of a school is to talk to students and alumni.

The unspoken rule here is: Be competitive, but don't look that way.
Medical student, University of California at San Francisco

- **Diversity.** In the past ten years, medical schools have been making concerted efforts to diversify their student bodies. The number of women students has risen so that in several schools there are an equal or greater number of women attending. However, there are still relatively few women faculty members, although that number has been steadily increasing too.

  Minority acceptances have also been on the rise. Most schools have special acceptance criteria and many have post-acceptance academic programs for under-represented minorities, which include African Americans, mainland Puerto Ricans, Mexican Americans, and Native Americans.

Taking the MCAT

The MCAT is a seven-hour test (including lunch and breaks) produced by the Association of American Medical Colleges, required by almost every medical school in the country. If you're a borderline student, a good score on the MCAT can help your chances of acceptance. If you don't do well on the MCAT, you may choose to take it more than once to improve your chances.

The test is divided into four sections: Physical Sciences, Biological Sciences, Verbal Reasoning, and a Writing Sample. The verbal and scientific sections are scored on a scale of one to fifteen, where one is low and fifteen is high. A score of ten or above is considered very good. The writing sample is scored on a scale of J-T, with T being the highest.

The science sections are designed to test your knowledge of basic concepts and problem-solving abilities in chemistry, biology, and physics. In the verbal reasoning section, you're given several reading passages, followed by questions based on the material just presented. This section is designed to evaluate your text comprehension abilities and reasoning skills. The writing sample, which evaluates writing and analytical skills, is comprised of two exercises. Each presents you with a short statement on a particular topic and asks you to write an essay about it.

Studying for the MCAT should be taken seriously. Some students feel that, because they've learned the material in their college classes, they don't need to review. But the material on the MCAT is based on introductory level courses, and the earliest you can take the test is your junior year in college, so two years may have passed since you reviewed the material being covered.

There are two ways to prepare for the MCAT—on your own, and with professional help. There are a number of review books available that suggest test-taking strategies and offer sample exams, including The Princeton Review's *Cracking the MCAT*. The second method of preparation is to take a review course, such as the one offered by The Princeton Review.

Here are some sample MCAT questions:

Part I: Verbal Reasoning, for which you are given 1 hour, 25 minutes

The following is a portion of a reading passage and a multiple-choice question based on the material:

> "Socialization" refers to the processes and dynamics by which children come to understand their position in relation to the positions of others. In the process of socialization, the child learns to respect the rights and property of others. Ideally, he or she recognizes, gradually, the need to control impulses and appetites, to accept and fulfill responsibilities, and to conform behavior to the circumstances that surround him or her at any given time. The six-month-old infant taken by a parent to the theater does not think it inappropriate to cry loudly during the performance, but the six-year-old will likely restrain himself even if he is uncomfortable and discontented.

1. The author probably compares the situations of a six-month-old and six-year-old taken to the theater in order to demonstrate that:
   A. fully socialized adults must take responsibility for less socialized children.
   B. children who are exposed to music and art will experience faster maturation.
   C. older children have greater appreciation for culture than do younger children.
   D. an older child is likely to be more socialized than a younger child.

In this example, **D** is the correct answer. In the passage, the author makes the point: "In the process of socialization, the child learns to respect the rights and property of others" and tells you that socialization is the ability to "conform behavior to the circumstances that surround" a person at any given time. In this passage, the illustration involving the theater supports the point that an older child is better able than a younger child to "conform behavior to the circumstances," and is therefore better socialized than a younger child.

Part II: Physical Sciences, for which you are given 1 hour, 40 minutes

This section has groups of multiple-choice questions based on preceding descriptive passages, and freestanding questions related neither to a passage nor to each other. Here are two examples of freestanding questions:

1. When an electron is added to a neutral atom to form its anion, the atomic radius:
   A. decreases, because the added electron makes the orbital more complete.
   B. increases, because the effective nuclear charge decreases.
   C. increases, because the electronegativity of the atom decreases.
   D. stays the same, because the added electron contributes negligible mass to the atom.

2. Three mechanical waves of frequencies 3 Hz, 5 Hz, and 7 Hz are passed through the same medium at equal velocities. The magnitudes of their respective displacement are 1, 2, and 4. What is the smallest possible displacement in the medium that could be caused by the resultant wave?
   A. 0
   B. 1
   C. 7
   D. 8

The answer to question number one is **B**. If you review periodic trends, you'll learn that atomic size reflects effective nuclear charge. The added electron will decrease effective nuclear charge, which will increase atomic radius.

The answer to question number two is also **B**. The superposition of any number of waves with differing frequencies and amplitudes will result in a complex wave. To solve this problem, you need to add the displacements caused by individual waves at each point in such a way as to create the smallest possible resulting displacement. (Or it could be the greatest possible destruction.) This will result from adding: $4 - (1 + 2) = 1$.

Part III: Writing Sample, for which you are given 60 minutes (separately timed at 30 minutes each)

In this section you are asked to consider a short statement and then given instructions as to the type of essay you are to write. Here is an example of a statement and its instructions:

> Consider this statement:
>
> **People get the government they deserve.**
>
> Write a unified essay in which you perform the following tasks: Explain what you think the above statement means. Describe a specific situation in which people do not get the government they deserve. Discuss what you think determines whether or not people get the government they deserve.

Obviously, there are no right or wrong answers in this section. The test reviewers are looking to see that you address all of the assigned tasks, that your essay is well conceived and well organized, and that you give the topic serious consideration.

Part IV: Biological Sciences, for which you are given 1 hour, 40 minutes

As in the Physical Sciences section, you are given certain groups of multiple choice questions, each preceded by a descriptive passage.

Other questions are freestanding, related neither to a passage nor to each other. Here are two examples of freestanding questions:

1. Sickle-cell anemia is a blood disorder due to a point mutation in a single gene. It is inherited as an autosomal recessive trait. A woman is heterozygous for the disorder, having one normal allele on the genome and one allele affected by the point mutation. She most likely has:
   A. full-blown sickle-cell anemia.
   B. sickle-cell trait, a carrier disease.
   C. no signs or symptoms of the disease.
   D. a predominance of sickle-shaped red blood cells.

2. Surgically implanted pacemakers are frequently used in the treatment of heart disease. Which of the following normal heart structures carries out the same functions as a pacemaker?
   A. The bundle of His
   B. The atrioventricular node
   C. The sinoatrial node
   D. The sinoventricular node

The answer to question number one is **B**. An individual with sickle-cell trait (as opposed to full-blown sickle-cell disease) has certain adverse symptoms associated with sickled blood cells, but she does not have fulminant sickle-cell anemia.

The answer to question number two is **C**. A review of mammalian physiology will tell you that the sinoatrial node generates the heartbeat and is thus known as the heart's natural "pacemaker."

The MCAT is given twice a year, in April and August. Most applicants are advised to take the MCAT in April of the year before they plan to attend medical school. That gives the schools enough time to receive your grades and gives you one more chance to take the test should you do poorly the first time.

The examination fee for the MCAT is $155. Registration packets are usually available at college premedical advisory offices, major university testing centers, or by writing to:

MCAT Program
P.O. Box 4056
Iowa City, IA 52243
(319) 337-1357

The Association of American Medical Colleges also runs a Fee Reduction Program through which financially disadvantaged individuals may take the MCAT for $55. To find out about this program, you can call the Section for Student Services, AAMC, at (202) 828-0600.

American Medical College Application Service (AMCAS)

There are two ways of applying to medical school. Only a handful of schools—those that are not members of the American Medical College Application Service (AMCAS)—ask you to apply to them directly. The majority of medical schools belong to AMCAS.

AMCAS allows you to fill out only one application instead of separate applications for each member school. Once you fill out an AMCAS application, it will be sent, along with your transcript and MCAT scores, to all the member schools you designate. The cost to you is determined by the number of member schools to which you are applying. You can obtain an AMCAS Application Request Card from your college premedical advisor, or by writing to AMCAS, Association of American Medical Colleges, Section for Student Services (2450 N Street, Suite 201, Washington, DC 20037-1131).

There are two basic parts of the AMCAS application. The first is a straightforward, fill-in-the-blanks account of your personal history. The second part, called "Your Personal Comments," allows you to talk about yourself, explain why you want to go to medical school, and express your views on becoming a doctor. If there are any problem areas on your transcript (that D you're hoping they won't notice) or any blank spots on your resume (those two years after college you spent watching TV and scooping frozen yogurt), you can explain them in the essay. On a more serious note, if you got low grades your sophomore year, you might use this essay to explain that there was a death in the family during your sophomore year, or that financial difficulties made it necessary for you to work long hours and drop one science class, which you made up in summer school.

This section of the application is less important than most students think. Many applicants spend months composing this essay, and are never satisfied with the results. However, consider these comments from the Chairman of the Committee on Admissions of one of the most prestigious medical schools in the country:

> *I would say that of all the components of the application process, the personal essay is probably the least useful. Applicants like to think, "Here's my chance. I may not look very different from thousands of other applicants on paper, but I know there's some golden combination of words out there. If I can just discover them, I'll captivate the reader's attention and get invited for an interview." Unfortunately, that's not the way it happens. There just aren't that many variations on "Why I Want to Become a Doctor."*
>
> *My advice? Keep it simple. Don't try to get too exotic or flowery. Don't worry if it sounds like everybody else's. The simplest approach is usually the best.*

That doesn't mean you can be sloppy or thoughtless in your essay. Admissions officers look to see that it is written clearly and logically, and that it does not contain errors. Before you write your essay, make an outline of what you want to say. Then write one or two drafts, and have an objective party review it for you. Once you've written your final version, have someone proofread it.

More often than not, the personal statement contributes negatively to the evaluation, either because the grammar is faulty or because it sounds patently insincere or contrived. Admissions officers are not looking for great wit or deep profundity; they simply want to get a brief glimpse of who you are and how you think.

Letters of Recommendation

Unlike your personal essay, letters of recommendation are one of the most influential aspects of your application to medical school. A borderline student is often pushed over into the acceptance pile because of excellent recommendations.

You must take the initiative in getting these letters. Forms are not included in your AMCAS application; you must submit separate letters to each school to which you are applying. Most schools require at least three letters of recommendation, but it's usually a good idea to get four or five, in case one is lost or is submitted late.

You'll need at least one, and possibly two, recommendations from science professors. Admissions officers don't want letters that simply reiterate your background and academic accomplishments. They read these letters to get insight into your character and integrity, your motivation, your self-discipline, and your leadership potential.

Therefore, it's to your advantage to get to know your professors. Ask questions in class and after class. Find out if you can participate in any research projects. If you take an introductory course with someone you like in your freshman year, try to take that professor's advanced level course as a junior or first semester senior, when you'll be asking for recommendations.

When you ask people for letters of recommendation, tactfully ask if they feel they can write about you in a way that will help you get accepted to medical school. If they feel they don't know you well enough, or cannot write an enthusiastic letter, thank them politely and ask someone else. When you find people who are willing to write you a letter, give them a list of the schools to which you are applying and the deadlines for sending such letters. Also provide them with stamped envelopes addressed to the appropriate schools. And don't forget to send thank-you notes once the letters are written.

The Interview

If you receive an invitation for an interview at a medical school, it means you've made the first cut, and are being considered seriously for acceptance. It is not a guarantee, as schools interview many more people than they can accept.

The interview is extremely important. If you make a bad impression, it can cancel out your good grades and excellent MCAT scores. If you make a good impression, however, it can raise your chances of acceptance dramatically. So comb your hair. Wear a suit. Smile. And prepare.

The advice for a successful interview is the same as the advice for your personal essay—keep it simple. Be honest; be yourself. You will be asked many questions. Some will be questions you've answered many times before, such as "Why do you want to be a doctor?" and "What do you plan to specialize in?" Some may be bizarre and outlandish, such as "Would you give up a body part to gain entrance to medical school?" Some may be controversial, such as "What should a physician's role be in the politics of abortion?"

Some questions may be highly personal, such as "Why aren't you married?" or "Why did you get divorced?" If this were a job interview, such questions would be illegal. As it is, they may seem inappropriate and make you angry or uncomfortable. How you handle this situation is up to you. Many students choose to answer the questions as calmly and briefly as possible. You can even change the subject. For instance, if asked about your divorce, you might say, "Every divorce is complicated, with mistakes made on both sides. Mine was no different. By the way, there's a question I wanted to ask you about this program...." Remember, you don't have to answer every question. If a question makes you truly uncomfortable, you have the right to decline to answer politely.

The truth is that interviewers are less interested in your actual answers than in how you handle yourself in the interview. They know that, as a doctor, you will often find yourself in stressful situations, and you must be able to retain a calm demeanor and your critical-thinking abilities. If you can't do this in an interview, how will you handle an emergency?

There are certain steps you can take to enhance your chances of a successful interview:

- **Practice.** Have people you know conduct mock interviews. Afterwards, ask them for their honest opinions about how you did. Did you come across effectively? Were your responses appropriate and sincere? What did you do if you were asked a question and didn't know the answer? Were you friendly? Confident? There are two things you should definitely avoid when going on interviews: First, don't memorize answers to questions. If you give a canned answer, it always sounds rehearsed and insincere. Second, don't try and give answers you *think* the interviewer wants to hear. Answer questions as honestly as possible, and if you don't know the answer to a question, say so.

- **Be prepared.** Go back over your resume, your school transcript, and any other personal history the interviewer may have read about you. If you've worked on research projects, be sure you can explain your methods and results. Read the school catalog. Talk to current and former students if possible. All interviewers think that their schools are unique and have something special to offer. They want to know that you think so, too.

- **Ask questions.** Although your main purpose at an interview is to get accepted into the school, you can also use this opportunity to decide if the school is right for you. Use this chance to find out more about the school and the particular programs it offers. Prepare a list of your most important questions before you get to the interview.

- **Get there early.** Be sure you have clear directions to the interview site and have allowed enough time for transportation snafus. Being late for an interview creates a bad impression, even if you have a good excuse.

- **Neatness counts.** Dress as if you were going for a corporate interview. You want to be evaluated on your personality and your qualifications, not on your loud jacket or mile-high hair.

- **Relax.** Interviewers expect a certain amount of nervousness. But they also expect that you will be confident enough to control your nerves and conduct yourself in a professional manner. If you're asked a controversial question, state your answer briefly and honestly. If you don't understand a question, ask for clarification. Make eye contact. Don't try to judge how the interview is going while you're in the midst of the experience. Many students are shocked to find out they've been accepted to schools after they thought they'd given a terrible interview.

- **Send a thank-you note.** No matter how you think the interview went, send the interviewer a brief, but personal, thank-you note.

As the Chairman of the Committee on Admissions quoted earlier told us:

> *The most important thing we look for is motivation and desire. It's hard to know how much anyone wants to become a doctor— there is no numerical score that quantitates motivation. But it's something we always look for.*
>
> *You've got to really want to become a doctor. It's not an easy process. It's a wonderful, life-enhancing experience—but it demands a lot from you. You have to work hard. You have to learn a lot. You have to have real faith that it's all worthwhile and it's all to a good end. If you have that, it will make things a lot easier for you.*

One of the questions interviewers always ask themselves at an interview is: "If I were sick, is this the sort of person I would like to have as my own doctor?" If the answer is yes, you are one substantial step closer to acceptance.

CHAPTER 2

Getting Started: Making the Transition

THE PRACTICALITIES

The Question of Money

Congratulations! You've been accepted to medical school. You've jumped the first major hurdle. There are, however, a number of decisions still to be made and some important challenges still to be met.

The biggest challenge you'll inevitably face, and the first question you'll probably ask yourself is: How am I going to pay for this? There is no getting around it—going to medical school is an expensive proposition. Almost every medical student requires financial assistance to complete his or her education. In 1994, the average medical student incurred debts of about $64,000. On the other hand, physicians are among the highest-paid professionals; currently the average physician earns over $160,000 annually.

These figures are constantly changing, however. Government cuts are making less money available for funding education. More and more physicians are going into salaried positions or family care practices, where earnings are lower. In any case, it will be many years before you reach your earning potential. Financial decisions you make now will affect you for many years to come, so they should be made with great care and thought.

There are two types of financial aid available: loans and scholarships. Loans need to be repaid, scholarships don't. In some cases, the amount of money available to you through a loan or a scholarship depends on your financial situation. In other cases, money is awarded to you no matter what your financial status.

There are four basic types of aid available:

Federal

Most students apply for federally-funded loans as their first option. Most of these loans are need-based, but some higher interest loans are available regardless of financial circumstances. Both undergraduate and medical school financial aid offices can provide information on them.

State

In order to qualify for these loans, you must be a resident of the state in which you're attending medical school. Loans are usually need-based. Contact the school's financial aid office and your state's department of education for information.

Institutional

This is aid that comes from the school itself, and varies greatly from one school to another. Contact the school's financial aid office for information.

Private

These loans and scholarships are funded by various corporations, religious groups, community organizations, foundations, and associations. Much of this aid is aimed at specific groups, such as minority or disadvantaged students, women, or students who want to practice family medicine in underserved areas. Information on these programs can be found in public, undergraduate, and medical school libraries.

Explore all your options. Since every medical school has its own policies and procedures regarding financial aid, your first step should be to contact the school's financial aid office, no matter what type of funding you're looking for. If you can arrange to get to the school, try to set up a one-on-one interview with a financial aid officer. Whether or not you can get there in person, be sure you get all the necessary information so that you have all the proper forms, are aware of important deadlines, and can weigh your various options.

If you were a fan of the television show "Northern Exposure," you know that there is also some funding available in exchange for services after graduation. The upside is that your education is paid for; the downside is that you are often required to pay back your support in inner-city or rural areas of the country. In "Northern Exposure," Dr. Joel Fleischman ended up in beautiful downtown Sicely, Alaska, as repayment for the financial aid he received in medical school. But your circumstances might not be so picturesque. And there probably won't be a TV crew filming you. Carefully consider how well you'd do in a remote rural area or a tough inner-city neighborhood.

These service-based scholarships, both state and federally funded, are in high demand, so if you're interested, you'll have to apply early.

USUHS is one of the best-kept secrets in medical education. It's the only school in the country where students are paid to attend medical school. Not only are the benefits great, the quality of the education is unbeatable!
Medical student, Uniformed Services University of Health Sciences

---

The following publications may also provide you with helpful information:

The Student Guide
Department of Education
Federal Student Aid Information
P.O. Box 84
Washington, DC 20044

Medical Scholarship and Loan Fund Program
American Medical Association
535 North Dearborn Street
Chicago, IL 60610

Informed Decision-Making: Part I, Financial Planning and Management for Medical Students; Part II: Sources of Financial Assistance for Medical School
National Medical Fellowships, Inc.
Scholarship Department
254 West 31 Street
New York, NY 10001

The Health Field Needs You! Sources of Financial Aid Information
Bureau of Health Professionals
Health Resources and Service Administration
Dept. Of Health and Human Services
Parklawn Building
5600 Fishers Lane
Rockville, MD 20857

Remember that tuition isn't the only cost involved when calculating how much money you'll need for your medical school education. You'll also have to pay for books, equipment, food, insurance, transportation, and housing. These additional costs may in some cases equal, or even exceed, the price of tuition.

Be sure you apply for financial aid early. Both you and your parents (even if you are living independently or are married) should file your income taxes as soon after January 1st as possible. Funds are often distributed on a first-come, first-served basis. If you are late in applying because of missing information, there may be no money left for you.

Finding a Place to Live

Housing situations vary depending on the school. Some schools offer dorm-style on-campus housing. Others have no on-campus housing at all. Some schools offer married student housing. And even if school-sponsored housing is available, you may choose to live elsewhere. There are several factors to consider:

Cost

Weigh the costs carefully. In some cases, on-campus housing is the most expensive option, and you might be able to save money by renting an apartment off-campus. However, you must then take into account any transportation costs you will incur, whether that means buying a car or utilizing public transportation. In some urban areas apartments are high-priced, so many students choose to have roommates to share expenses.

Study habits

Do you need total silence and no disturbances when you study? Then dorm life may not be the best option for you. On the other hand, if study groups are more your style, on-campus housing may make group participation easier.

Commuting, parking, and public transportation

How far from campus do you have to go to find affordable housing? If you need to drive to school, is there adequate parking? Do you have to pay for parking privileges? And if you don't have a car, is public transportation an option? How safe is it? How much time will commuting add to your already overloaded schedule? If commuting cuts dramatically into your study or relaxation time, it may be worth it to spend more money and live on or close to campus.

Ask the school's admissions officer about the percentage of students who live on and off campus. If there is on-campus housing available, yet most students find their own housing, there's probably a good reason. Or, if ninety percent of the students live on-campus, there must be a clear advantage.

Of course, the best information comes from students and alumni. They can tell you the pros and cons of on- and off-campus living.

- Students at George Washington University School of Medicine and Health Science, Georgetown University School of Medicine, and Howard University, all located in Washington, DC, rate off-campus living highly. Housing is expensive but plentiful, and DC has an outstanding mass transit system.

- On-campus housing at Northwestern University Medical School in Chicago received enthusiastic reviews, but students warn that there is a significant difference in quality between the school's two residence halls. As for off-campus housing, you might have trouble finding an affordable apartment in the school's posh neighborhood, but there is an easily accessible, and relatively safe, public transportation system.

- The University of Louisville School of Medicine offers several different styles of on-campus housing, and students reported that there were also plenty of reasonably priced off-campus rental units available.

- At the University of Texas Medical School at Houston, parking is such a major problem it was mentioned by every student interviewed. The University offers apartments a short distance from campus, but the school recently shut down its shuttle service. One sophomore said, "You have a choice of either parking in a nearby public garage and paying out the butt for it, or paying a fortune to park miles from campus and waiting forty-five minutes for a bus."

Don't wait until the last minute to make housing decisions. The best accommodations go fast. If you have friends or acquaintances in the area, ask them for advice on the safety and financial factors of various neighborhoods. Ask if you can sleep on their couches while you look for an apartment. If you do have to commute to school, use the time productively. Perhaps you can carpool with other students and become a traveling study group.

Summer School Pros and Cons

Many schools offer incoming students the option of taking an introductory biochemistry or anatomy course during the month before the first year begins. Although you might prefer to spend these months as your last summer of freedom, committing to a summer course at the medical school has its benefits. If you have been accepted into the school under special circumstances (such as a program for the educationally disadvantaged), you may be required to take these courses before the regular term begins. If you did not take biochemistry or anatomy in college, you may want to take them now. Since the courses given during the first year of medical school usually assume some basic knowledge of these subjects, you may find yourself overwhelmed if you have to learn the introductory information as well. And if you have been out of school for several years, you may want to take these summer classes to get back into the "school mode" so that you won't feel quite so disoriented when the regular session begins.

Any stress or anxiety you may feel about moving to a new place and adjusting to a new phase of your life can be worked out during the summer session, leaving you better prepared to begin regular classes. You'll also have an opportunity to meet some of your classmates early instead of wading through a sea of strange faces at orientation.

Orientation

I remember the first day. It was all paperwork, signing this, signing that, one line after another. No one knew each other. It was weird, and it stayed weird for the first month or so. You don't know where you fit in. You're in class with five percent of the country's best students, and you just keep asking yourself, "Do I really belong here?"

Resident, Geisinger Medical Center

Orientation to medical school, as in most other schools, can leave you feeling more disoriented than anything else. If you look at it as an adventure, rather than as a grueling experiment in wasted time and forced togetherness, you'll be able to relax and enjoy it. Take comfort from the fact that everyone there is going through the same first-day jitters. And you will actually get some useful information, so it's a good idea to pay attention.

If you haven't been to summer classes, orientation gives you the opportunity to meet your classmates, as well as some of the returning students. Pick their brains for key suggestions and advice about the coming year. Second-year students can be the very best source for all kinds of important information and tidbits, from which books to buy to which local pizza place is the best. Take them out; buy them their favorite beverages. You'll learn a lot.

Getting Organized and Setting Priorities

If you've never been organized before in your life, now is a good time to get started. Time is always a precious commodity, but it is even more so during your years in medical school. There is a lot to be accomplished, but there are still only twenty-four hours in the day. If you are disorganized and don't learn to set priorities, stress will be the overriding factor in your entire medical school experience. On the other hand, if you set up workable systems for yourself early on, your anxiety level will decrease dramatically.

The systems you set up need not be complicated. The "to-do list" is a simple tool that can make a world of difference in a day in the life of a medical student. Some people keep a running list which they are constantly updating. Others prefer to make a new list every day. Either way, prepare your list each night before you go to bed. When you wake up, you'll be fresh and focused, and you'll know what needs to be done that day. Your list can include everything from the urgent to the mundane—reminding yourself to do laundry or to send a birthday card to Mom can keep you from feeling buried in the minutiae.

Every medical student faces the same dilemma: how to make the best and most productive use of time. If you constantly feel pressured, if you're always worrying about all that you have yet to accomplish, you won't be able concentrate on the task at hand. That's why time management is an absolutely essential skill for a successful medical school career. Time management is based on organization, priority, and focus.

- Organize your tasks so that they fall into a logical sequence. This frees up your time so that you're not always running around asking yourself, "What should I do next?" You have a plan for the day, the week, and/or the month. When you organize your tasks, you can stop berating yourself (as we all do) for not doing what you think you "should" be doing.

- Prioritize your activities so that what *must* get done does get done. Some activities are more urgent than others. List your activities in terms of importance; that way, if some less important things don't get done, they can be shifted to another day without affecting your overall productivity.

- Focus on the activity that is most important right now. After you've organized and prioritized, pay attention to the task at hand and give it 100 percent until you're ready to move on to the next activity. That includes recreation and relaxation; both your mind and body need time to rest and rejuvenate. If you haven't organized and prioritized, you'll always be wondering if there's something more important you should be doing.

The most important rule in time management is this: Don't let anyone tell you there is only one way to manage your time. Devise a system that works for you, and keep it simple.

Each of us has unique, individual priorities. Purchase a daily planner or notebook in which you can keep your schedule. Write down how you plan to spend each day, and be sure to incorporate every aspect of your school schedule, including classes, labs, and exams, as well as adequate time to study. Then allocate time for those individual activities you have promised yourself, including time for your significant other, spouse, and/or children, time to participate in sports or hobbies of interest to you, and time to socialize with friends. Unless you have written down a practical schedule, you will constantly be wondering where the time has gone and why you have not gotten to one thing on your to-do list.

Learning (or Re-learning) How to Study

As soon as classes begin, you'll realize why organization is essential to success in medical school. It is a vital tool for creating and maintaining the study habits you'll need for the next two years. Whether you come in as a freshman directly after graduating college, or have been away from school for several years, medical school offers a series of challenges to your study skills. Certainly your college or post-college preparation courses in the sciences will help, but the volume of the material and the speed at which you are expected to absorb it will probably be something that you have not encountered before.

There are two major mistakes med students make. One is establishing a pattern of waiting until the last minute to study a particular subject, and then consuming quarts of caffeine and textbooks full of information the night before exams. The second is the tendency to read every single word on every single page of a textbook chapter on which they're going to be tested. Neither method will enable you to learn all the material that will be covered. Knowing which areas are most important will enable you to spend your time wisely without getting buried in the details.

Don't fall behind. Keeping up with the pace of your classes, labs, and your small group courses will definitely pay off in the end. "How can I do that?" you may be gasping. There is no one answer to that question. Develop and combine different study methods available to suit your own style and needs. You may choose to schedule time to read the syllabus material or the textbook chapter the night before the subject will be covered in a lecture. The lecture will then serve as a review. Some people find it easier to attend the lecture first and reinforce the material by reading and reviewing the textbook chapter or syllabus notes that evening.

Because so much of surviving the first two years of medical school depends on memorizing volumes of material, it's critical to develop a reliable system of memorization that works for you. Flash cards with a term on one side and the definition (or other information relating to that term) on the other side are effective for many students. They can be especially efficient for students who commute and use commuting time to study the easily portable flash cards. Keep your flash cards in a small file card box organized by topic so that they will be easily accessible for later reference. You'll be grateful for this organization once you reach both the national boards and the clinical years, as all of your preclinical course materials will be at your fingertips.

Sleep, Diet, and Exercise

Although you'll probably never put "sleep" on your to-do list or weekly schedule, it might not be a bad idea. Each of us has his own sleep requirements for optimal daily performance, usually ranging from six to eight hours per night. Try to arrange your schedule so that you can get the number of hours you need. It is a fallacy that one can make up lost sleep over the weekend; cumulative sleep deprivation will sap your strength much sooner than you realize.

Poor diet and lack of nutritional fortification will also take a toll. So eat balanced meals, including all the food groups—not just pizza, coffee, and vending machine snack foods. Buy pre-peeled carrots, boxes of raisins, or granola bars and carry them with you for quick energy boosts. Maintaining a healthy diet will help reduce anxiety and increase energy.

Another energy booster is exercise. For many medical students, the only exercise they get is walking from one class to another. Exercise not only increases energy, it improves your overall well-being and self-esteem. And it can serve as an effective release for tension and frustration.

One medical student we spoke to had always wanted to run the New York Marathon. He trained the entire summer between his first and second years of medical school for the November race. "I was working on a research project at the time and devoted the remainder of the summer to running," he said. "By the time the race approached I was in the best shape I'd ever been in, physically and mentally. Because my training schedule was so regimented, my entire life became that way, including my study habits. Not only did I never fall behind in my schoolwork, but on marathon day I ran my own personal best!"

Another student's favorite study breaks were the 11:00 p.m. soccer games he played as a member of an intramural medical school indoor soccer league. "We had so much fun working up a serious sweat at that hour," he told us, "and study sessions seemed to whiz by if I knew I was going to play a game later. I became much more efficient with my time and got some of the best nights' sleep I've ever had."

School Activities and Medical Associations

Just as in college, medical schools often have special interest clubs, ranging from the Emergency Medicine Club or the Psychiatry Club to the Hiking and Biking Club. If you have a special interest that you know you share with others or would like to introduce on your own, the Student Affairs Office is usually more than happy to help you design a new activity club. These activities offer a chance to break up the days and provide an opportunity for socializing with your classmates other than in the lab.

One medical student attributes his improved classroom performance and his reduced level of study-related anxieties to his involvement in the school-affiliated martial arts team. "I have martial arts to thank for surviving medical school," he said. "In addition to belonging to a group of people who shared my interest in this form of exercise and relaxation, I learned to control my anxiety and remain level-headed throughout the four years. Not only did I receive my M.D. from my medical school, I got my black belt there as well."

Medical schools also offer the opportunity to become involved in various administrative committees, such as the curriculum committee or the promotional committee. These organizations give you a chance to get to know faculty committee members as well as other important members of your school's administration, such as the Dean of Students. Such connections can make it easier to approach these people with questions or problems, and often provide access to potential mentors.

Many schools also sponsor community outreach programs. For instance, a first-year medical student who is a member of STATS (Students Teaching AIDS to Students) told us: "I really look forward to my trips into the local community high schools. It's such a blast to be able to spend time with the kids, and I really feel good about my purpose as an educator in AIDS prevention. My favorite part is the reaction I get from the students when I demonstrate how to put on a condom, using a banana as a model. I realized that if I could go through with that demonstration in front of fifty high school students, nothing would phase me as a doctor!"

Another popular activity is participation in the American Medical Student Association (AMSA). There are many special interest committees and sub-committees within this national organization. If you enjoy being politically active, AMSA provides opportunities to run for elective offices and discuss medical school policies and national health problems. You also have the option of joining the American Medical Association (AMA). Although not specifically geared to the medical student, the AMA will provide you with valuable information about the medical profession at large. There are several other national medical organizations that may be of interest, including the American Medical Women's Association (AMWA). A list of these organizations should be available in your school library.

Get a Life: Medical School and Personal Relationships

I feel very fortunate to have my wife here. We have a life outside of medicine. Once in a while it's just nice to come home and be with someone who's not in medical school. It clears your head and makes it easier to get through.
Resident, Geisinger Medical Center

Whether you realize it or not, during your medical school years you'll come to depend on your personal relationships, including your significant other, your children, your siblings, your parents, your grandparents, and your friends for moral support, ego boosting, and that occasional back rub after a long day of studying. Maintaining these relationships takes work. It may be difficult to come home to a partner who's looking forward to spending quality time with you when you're exhausted from a day of classes, labs, and intensive study. Remember that the changes that are affecting your life as a medical student are affecting your family's lives as well.

"It's an ongoing struggle," the wife of a medical student told us. "You both go through a lot of changes. You start to think, 'Is it worth it?' There are a lot of sacrifices and a lot less intimacy. I tried to be supportive, but there were times when it was hard to get my own needs met.

"You get married for the companionship, and you just don't have as much of that when your spouse is in medical school. You have to learn to adjust. Have your own life. Learn to be independent. Be able to entertain yourself, and make friends you can hang around with. Sometimes your spouse is so wrapped up in the medical world, you feel totally left out. It's important to get your spouse to share what happened during the day so you can feel a part of it, too."

Whatever you do, make sure that you protect your important relationships. Realize that there will be difficult times, but that it's possible to get through them. Offer support to those in your life just as you expect and need support from them. It may be difficult for others to understand your time pressures, but if you take the time to explain your circumstances, they'll be much more tolerant of your need for study time.

Take advantage of the friendships you develop in medical school. People who are going through the same experience as you can form a wonderful support network, especially during rough times. When one first-year student's father died suddenly of a myocardial infarction, he wondered how he was going to get through that time without falling apart. "My dad died just at the time that my class was starting a course in cardiovascular physiology," he told us. "Everything I heard and read seemed to remind me of his death. Thankfully I had established some really close friends in my medical school group, and they were extremely supportive and available to me. Now, when I think of my dad's early death, I remember how proud he was of me for choosing to become a doctor. Perhaps I will have the opportunity some day to prevent heart disease and an early death of one of my own patients."

Pitfalls: Stress, Fatigue, Anxiety, Depression, and Substance Abuse

For the most part, medical school is a richly rewarding experience. But there are times when the pressure builds, and it is our goal to help you find healthy ways of coping. It's important to address those circumstances that may impede your success. The first and most important step is the early detection of anything that threatens to interfere with your ability to perform well as a medical student or anywhere else in your life. The next and equally important step is finding help when you need it.

Feeling stress and/or fatigue can wreak havoc on your emotional and physical well-being. Certain amounts of stress and fatigue are an inevitable part of the medical school experience. But when they seem to get the best of you and become your whole existence, something must be done. Allowing yourself more time for exercise, recreation, and relaxation often helps.

However, extreme stress and fatigue may disguise more serious conditions such as generalized anxiety or depression (which you will study in psychopathology and in your third-year psychiatry clerkship). It's important to realize that these conditions are two of the most common psychological reactions to stress. Both are treatable with therapy and/or anti-depressant medications.

Another common problem among medical students and health care professionals is substance abuse. Beware of your own vulnerability. Needless to say, it's difficult to successfully survive medical school when your life is complicated by alcohol or drugs. Many schools sponsor student/faculty-run counseling programs, such as Aid for Impaired Medical Students, which provide a confidential, protective system for students in need of help. The school's mental health center can also be a good source of support and guidance.

Sometimes getting through medical school, especially the first two years, seems like an impossible task. On the other hand, it's really very structured; it's all set out for you. You go to classes, you read a large amount, you take the test, and then you're finished. If you work hard, if you learn to budget your time and set priorities, you can just roll with it.

Associate professor, Albany Medical College

CHAPTER 3

The First Year

WHAT YOU CAN EXPECT

Medical school is a journey filled with highs and lows. Sometimes you will feel excited and exhilarated. Other times you will feel frustrated and overwhelmed. If you know what to expect beforehand, you'll be better able to handle the good as well as the bad.

As medicine enters the 21st century, the field is undergoing a major overhaul. The practice of medicine itself is changing; at the same time we're seeing changes in the types of people who are becoming doctors, as well as changes in the way they're being trained. The applicant pool to medical schools has changed considerably in the past ten years. No longer is the average applicant a science major who has just graduated from college. Many applicants now bring with them backgrounds in the humanities, the social sciences, and the arts. Many of them are coming back to school after having taken time off from their studies to pursue other interests. And more and more students have spent several years working in other fields only to decide later that they really want a career in medicine.

Medical school is changing as well. Until the 1980s, medical schools all followed the same structural formula: the first two years of study consisted of classwork taught in large, teacher-directed lectures on the basic sciences. The second two years concentrated on clinical experience—primarily working with patients in hospital settings.

For over a decade, many schools have been trying to close the gap between classroom study with its large amount of rote memorization, and the hands-on learning of clinical experience. Some schools have eliminated the traditional lecture in favor of small-group, problem-based learning, and are introducing patient contact early in the first year. Most schools are in transition, reforming their curricula a little more each year.

Though styles of teaching may be changing, you will still be studying the basic sciences during your first two years. These traditional science courses will help you learn the language of medicine and form a foundation of knowledge that will be important throughout your entire career. Basic sciences are readily applicable in the hospital setting. For example, principles learned in microbiology have practical value in understanding infectious disease. Similarly, grasping the concepts involved in cardiac physiology will help you recognize and diagnose patients with heart problems. The better you know the basic sciences, the easier it will be to understand clinical medicine.

Courses covered during your first year include anatomy, histology/embryology, biochemistry, physiology, neuroscience, and behavioral science.

INTO THE CLASSROOM

Teaching Styles

Basic science courses are taught by various methods including lectures, labs, and small discussion groups. Lectures are usually held in a large auditorium with a professor presiding. The professor will discuss a topic for about one hour with the aid of a slide projector. Each professor has a different style of teaching; some distribute handouts, making note-taking unnecessary. Others speak quickly, fail to enunciate, and neglect to provide any type of handout (many basic science professors are paid for their research, and not their teaching abilities). Some tell awful jokes. Laugh if you are sitting in the front row. If you're *sure* the professor can't see you and doesn't know your voice, you may groan. **Do not** copy the joke into your notes. Some students will do this. Laugh at them. You will not be tested on jokes, bad or otherwise.

In lectures, we get too much information too fast. They feed it to us and we spit it out. It's just regurgitation. The small-group learning they've been experimenting with is a lot better.... We learn to work as a team.
Medical student, Northwestern University

The Classroom

Going to lecture after lecture can make the day seem endless. Students can become depressed by a curriculum that sometimes schedules six lectures in a day. However, once clinical rotation begins, you will appreciate the knowledge gained in these lectures as you apply the basic sciences to the practice of medicine.

At the beginning, you will probably find that it is very difficult to take notes and digest the material being taught at the same time. To overcome these difficulties (and earn a buck), students sometimes take it upon themselves to organize a transcription service. By taping the lectures and later transcribing them from tape, students are able to concentrate on the material instead of frantically trying to write down what's being said. The notes are transcribed by participating members and handed out to all those paying the subscription fee.

Lab work also plays an integral part in first- and second-year courses. Students are usually divided into small groups for more individualized instruction in lab sessions. Lab work can include looking at slides, working on cadavers, and experimenting with animals. Topics are covered concurrently with lecture material, which gives students the opportunity to reinforce what is covered. Take advantage of lab time. It gives you "hands-on" learning, and you get to know your classmates. Some of your lab partners may turn out to be your closest friends in medical school.

The first courses we had were gross anatomy and cell biology. Gross anatomy is mostly in the lab; there's a lot of hands-on work. They broke us up into groups. I was with three other students. We developed a strong bond that we still have going.

Resident, Geisinger Medical Center

Group discussions allow students to interact with professors on a more personal level. In groups of ten to twenty people, students have the opportunity to ask questions and clarify material covered in lecture. Professors may use these sessions to quiz students. This might be terribly nerve-racking for some. After all, answering questions in front of the professor and your peers can be difficult. Impress your professors and fellow students by being prepared; this will help alleviate any fear and allow you to make the best use of these sessions. Group discussions can help you gauge your understanding of the subject, which then allows you to fine-tune your study habits accordingly.

Textbooks

No matter how a course is taught, textbooks provide a necessary supplement (see Appendix II). Incorporating the right textbooks into your course is crucial, but this can often be a difficult task. Some teachers try to make the job easier by recommending texts to use with their classes, but some recommended textbooks carry expensive price tags and are so lengthy that it is difficult to complete the reading within the assigned time period. There are always alternatives. Ask third- and fourth-year students at your school what to read. They are your best resource, as they have already successfully completed the courses you are now taking.

There are two types of books available: textbooks and review books. Textbooks (you're familiar with these) are usually large, comprehensive tomes with lengthy explanations about the subject area. If a step-by-step explanation is necessary for you to understand the material, and you are able to study the details without being overwhelmed by them, then a good textbook is for you. Review books offer complete but concise explanations of the subject areas. Reading a review book allows you to cover the material faster than if you were reading a textbook. Students have been successful using both types of books, so you must decide which is right for you. You may choose to study from textbooks in one subject, and review books in another, depending on your previous knowledge of the subject, your ability to grasp its concepts, and your personal study preferences.

Your goal is to gain knowledge and information from the courses you take. It doesn't matter if this is accomplished by attending lectures, organizing or subscribing to a note-taking service, or using a standard textbook. It's up to you to find the most effective tools to help you comprehend the material. Don't be upset if the first method you try doesn't work. Try something else until you develop your own learning style and embark on your own road to success.

First Year Courses

Anatomy

Some consider anatomy to be a student's true initiation to medical school. Others see it as the foundation of all medicine. Either way, it's important. Few would disagree that your first day of gross anatomy lab is one that you will never forget. It will probably be your first confrontation with a cadaver. Most students have never faced death so intimately, nor dealt with the feelings that go with it. Working with a dead body will bring out a variety of emotional responses, including fears about your own mortality. However, this course, more than any other, puts you in touch with the doctor's responsibility for the lives and deaths of other human beings.

Prior to your first day in anatomy, you will most likely be introduced to your cadaver, making the transition less anxiety-provoking. Through initial lecture courses, an introductory lab lecture, and opportunities to speak to second-year students who have completed the course, you should develop a level of comfort—and excitement—about the experience that lies ahead.

Most of the teaching in gross anatomy takes place in the laboratory, where you will dissect the cadaver. This course definitely emphasizes hands-on experience. Lectures supplement the lab, rather than the other way around. Due to the limited number of cadavers available, students must share a body; usually four to eight people will work together on one cadaver.

You will either be assigned to a group or have the opportunity to choose your partners. The choice of compatible partners is important, as you will be spending many long hours with them. Try to find people whose personalities mesh well with your own. If you are a serious person, find others who are also serious and will not distract you or detract from your intensity. If you are easygoing, find partners who share this trait.

Whether or not you have the luxury of choosing, it is crucial to work together as a team. Since you will be sharing a dead body (or one side of a body, depending on your school) with three or more other people, it is important to be organized. If the tasks and responsibilities are divided fairly among the group's members, your experience will be both more valuable and more enjoyable. Everyone should have an opportunity to dissect, to read the manual, and to look up information in the textbook and atlas.

After organizing your lab group, the next step is to purchase any equipment you need for lab, usually available through your school bookstore. Necessary equipment usually includes a dissection kit (one per group), a lab manual, an atlas, a textbook, a long white coat and a box of disposable latex gloves. Investing in an extra atlas for your group to share in anatomy lab is often worthwhile. No one wants to take an atlas smelling of formalin back home with her.

Wear appropriate clothes for anatomy lab (they don't have to be black): long pants, a long-sleeved shirt, a lab coat, and comfortable shoes that will properly support you standing for long periods of time. Your school will probably provide a locker in which you can keep your formalin-contaminated anatomy clothes and lab coat (chances are you will end up throwing them all into the garbage as you walk out of your final anatomy exam). Make sure you are warm enough; the lab rooms are often cool. Pull your hair back if it is long; trim your beard if you think it will be in the way. And remember, you can always wear two pairs of gloves to protect your hands from the smell of formalin. Don't be surprised if you feel the need to shower after each lab in order get that smell out of your hair. Definitely shower if you have a date later that evening.

Now that you are completely outfitted for your first day of anatomy lab, you can begin the academic preparation. You will find it helpful to review the section of anatomy scheduled for dissection prior to that lab day. Memorizing the material is not necessary, as an atlas is always available at your table, but having some prior understanding of it frees you to interact with your partners and professors and enhances your learning experience. Remember that you are a walking atlas, and you can always use your own body as a study tool—and you can be sure you'll never look at any part of your body in the same way again.

The first day is an unforgettable, even surreal, experience. The cadaver's head is wrapped in cloth and remains covered. Can you really be working on a human being? The smell of the formalin brings you quickly back to your senses, and you are ready for the first incision. Everyone is nervous on the first day of dissection. Before you can begin, however, your first order of business is to give the cadaver a name, and introduce yourself, an anatomy ritual. Doctors always introduce themselves to patients. Like any other person, the cadaver represents an individual and every individual has a name. Name it wisely.

Your cadaver is actually your first patient. You are the surgeon with the unique opportunity to perform surgery without any dire consequences or repercussions. There are no lethal errors in anatomy lab. Morbidity is zero.

You walk into a big room with the professors standing around in white coats, and bodies covered in white sheets. The room is very quiet. It's pretty intimidating. Then you realize you've got a human body there, someone who's donated their body to science for the specific purpose of giving you a gift so that you can learn how to be a doctor. It's so powerful, the first time you take a scalpel to a human body. And eventually, you're looking at a human heart and holding it in your hand. A human heart! It's simply awesome.

MD, Albany Medical Center

The first time you cut into human flesh will feel strange and awkward. Your hands will shake. Be assured, you will overcome this feeling. In the beginning, dissection will be slow and tedious; it can take hours (depending on the patient and your lab partners' confidence) to cut through those initial layers of skin and fat on some bodies. You don't need to have the hands of a neurosurgeon, however. Your dissection may never look as perfect as the one in the atlas; however, with time and practice your technique will improve dramatically.

A good way to review material is to go into the lab with your group after hours and study the cadaver in combination with your notes and atlas. Working late nights in the anatomy lab can be quite an experience. Being alone in a dimly lit room surrounded by dead bodies may remind you of scenes from *Friday the 13th*. Every year, some unfortunate medical student is the victim of someone's prank: In the lab alone at night, about to uncover a cadaver, the student is stunned to find the body rising on its own—only to discover, after several moments of panic, a practical joker under the sheet.

An additional study tool for your anatomy course is A.D.A.M.®, an interactive computer program that serves as both a three-dimensional atlas and a simulated cadaver. You can also study radiological images such as X rays or CT scans to increase your knowledge of anatomical perspectives.

Gross anatomy contains a huge amount of information; learning it all would take a lifetime. Your job is to learn the important information, not the minutiae. A systematic approach to studying the body will make this task easier. Remember that the material stressed in lab and lecture is the same material that is usually stressed on the exams. The lecture notes and lab manual, supplemented by an atlas, can be your best study guides.

There are all sorts of memorization tricks and tactics that have been developed over the years; mnemonics, poems, and songs are passed on through generations of medical students to help memorize anatomical terms. Some of them are hilarious, others are just plain silly, but all are unforgettable. If you have a creative bent, you can compose some of your own or design them together with your lab partners. Putting anything to a tune may be useful for the musically gifted and fun if you find a partner to harmonize with. Just make sure you don't break into song while taking your final exam.

The anatomy course itself is divided into several parts based on either anatomic systems or functions. You'll be tested on each section, and there will be a comprehensive final exam. Each test has a written component and a lab practical/oral; both contribute to your final grade.

There are as many approaches to gross anatomy as there are medical students. You may see this course as a difficult challenge you will be proud to have survived. Cadaver dissection or the vast memorization may seem distant from the work you imagine yourself enjoying as a physician. Or you might feel sure that your success as a student of anatomy will be crucial to your endeavors, particularly if you want to specialize in surgery, obstetrics/gynecology, radiology, or pathology.

Regardless of your approach, you will find that your experience in gross anatomy changes you. In the words of W. Somerset Maugham in *Of Human Bondage*, "You will have to learn many tedious things . . . which you forget the moment you have passed your final examination, but in anatomy it is better to have learned and lost than never to have learned at all."

Histology/Embryology

While anatomy provides you with a gross understanding of the human body, embryology and histology focus on the microscopic aspects. According to *Stedman's Medical Dictionary*, histology is "microanatomy: the science concerned with the minute structure of cells, tissues, and organs in relation to their function." Embryology is the "science of the origin and development of the organisms from fertilization of the ovum to extrauterine or extraovular life." Studying histology and embryology concurrently with anatomy will give you a better overall understanding of the human body.

The material covered in histology is not particularly difficult; the lecture topics are fairly straightforward, dealing with function and structure of cells that make up the body. Like anatomy, this course is divided into two sections, lab and lecture, but unlike anatomy, lab is not the focus of the course.

In lab, students are divided into small groups of ten to twenty people. Each session, you will have to look at a set of slides and/or electron micrographs and be able to identify structures and other relevant information. An atlas and an instructor will be available to help you with this task.

You will need to purchase or rent a microscope, oil immersion, and lens paper. The microscope is your main learning tool in histology lab. You will be exposed to innumerable slides in lecture, but most of your learning will take place through the eyepiece of your microscope.

The key to this course is being able to visualize microscopic structures, which will take time. Students sometimes have a hard time adjusting to the microscope; being able to look through the eyepiece and focus can prove difficult, if not impossible, at times. You will first distinguish various microscopic structures; then you will compare their sizes regardless of what magnification is being used. You'll learn that cells look different depending on the plane along which they were sliced. It will take time and practice to master these skills. Once, a student found an oddly shaped figure in his slide of skeletal muscle tissue. Thinking it was some type of parasite, he eagerly called the professor over to proclaim his magnificent discovery. The professor spent several minutes carefully examining the slide, and then asked for a handkerchief. After a few quick flicks of the wrist, the professor returned the microscope to the student, whose prize-winning discovery turned out to be have been a smudge on the eyepiece.

Unlike anatomy, a lab study group for histology is not essential. Reviewing available slides and kodachromes and incorporating them with your lecture notes will help you achieve a better understanding of the role cells play in human bodily functions. Review topics from lab and lecture together to keep memorization to a minimum and enhance your grasp of the material.

Exams in histology test information from both lab and lecture via written and practical sections. The lab practical will consist of a set of slide/electron micrograph unknowns that you must identify both under the microscope and as kodachromes.

Embryology is the study of human development that provides the link between microscopic and gross anatomy. It is a short course, incorporated with either histology or anatomy, in which you will trace the maturation of the human embryo from initial fertilization through full gestation. The professor will discuss topics and present slides that show the different stages of gestation to give you a perspective on human development.

Small group discussions are an integral part of the learning process. They represent an avenue for additional clarification of subjects discussed in lecture or an opportunity for students to present topics.

Histology and embryology, emphasizing the study of the cells, tissues, and organs that make up the human body, are the stepping stones to understanding the human structure. As with gross anatomy, visualization is the key. Incorporating these three areas of study will enable you to grasp the big picture. Building from each of these courses, you will develop a strong foundation from which you can attain higher levels of comprehension.

Biochemistry

Biochemistry is the study of the structures and reactions of the human body's cellular and tissue components, and the role molecular structures play in biological function. The course is mostly lectures, which will range from the interesting to the downright tiresome; some may leave you wondering what biochemistry has to do with patient care. However, understanding the chemical processes of the human body makes it easier to understand the mechanisms behind various treatments. This is especially important in knowing how, why, and where drugs work.

You will be given a tremendous amount of information at each lecture. You might feel overwhelmed. But you're reading this book, so you'll be okay! The key to succeeding in biochemistry is not just to memorize pathway after pathway of biochemical formulas; the trick is to reason out processes and pathways.

You can try to make the material more relevant (and interesting) when studying by correlating it with clinical facts. Some lecturers may neglect this, but you don't have to. For example, a biochemical defect of an amino acid can cause the disease of sickle-cell anemia. Associations like this can keep you from drowning in an endless sea of biochemical enzymes.

Keep up with the lecture material! Organizing it into different charts, each containing several pathways, can make the covered topics more manageable by allowing you to master them step by step. Make certain you know the following:

- the name of the pathway and its function in the cell
- the structures and names of the initial substrates and final products of the pathways
- type of pathway (synthetic vs. degradative)
- enzymes involved in the pathway
- location of the pathway in the cell/body
- key steps in the pathway

You'll be tested on these pathways and their individual components.

Lectures will be supplemented by group discussions and/or problem-solving sessions. Again, small groups provide an opportunity to meet with a professor on a more personal level and discuss and clarify topics relevant to the lectures. Problem-solving sessions give you a chance to apply lecture material to solve work problems. Group participation is encouraged and expected, so it is important to come prepared.

Sorry, but there are no shortcuts to learning the material in biochemistry. If you understand the concepts, memorization will be much easier. Don't forget those charts you made up throughout the course. Around exam time, they make for easy review.

Although biochemistry sometimes seems dry and abstract, with no clinical relevance, the material serves as a building block for other courses. Pharmacology and microbiology require an understanding of these biochemical concepts. In the meantime, if you keep up with the classwork and review the important material before each exam, you can keep from being overwhelmed.

Physiology

Physiology is your first glimpse of what real medicine is about; you will learn about the normal processes and functioning of the human body in everyday life. Through this course, you will begin to develop an understanding of how the body functions, such as why the heart pumps, how the lungs work, and how the stomach digests. By first mastering normal physiological processes, you can then develop an understanding of disease processes and abnormal functioning. This is the basis of all clinical medicine.

In this course, lecturers tend to use the blackboard as well as slides in presenting their talks. Physiology lectures are different from those of the other basic sciences because they are more conceptual. Professors use mathematical equations to help explain concepts; bring a calculator to class to help you follow along. This is crucial in discussing renal, pulmonary, and cardiac physiology.

Basic physiological principles are demonstrated in lab sessions, where clinical experiments make the lecture material come alive. Some schools use live animals to illustrate the functions of individual organ systems. Sometimes you are the subject of experiments that measure blood pressure and pulse rates.

I remember one lab session involving the respiratory system. That morning's lecture was to cover diseases of the lung. The professor brought in a machine that measures lung capacity. He stressed that harmful acts, like smoking, decrease the lung's ability to function effectively, which can often be demonstrated through decreased lung capacity. Both smokers and nonsmokers in the lab group volunteered to test the machine. To everyone's dismay—especially the professor's—the person with the greatest lung capacity was a student with a two-pack-a-day habit. It only served to prove, once again, that there are no hard and fast rules in medicine.

Resident, Sloan Kettering Memorial Hospital

Problem-solving sessions provide a crucial addition to physiology lectures. Here you have the opportunity to increase your comprehension of physiological concepts by applying them to clinical scenarios. Professors also use this time to review difficult topics and resolve any questions you may have. Because much of the material in physiology is abstract, it can be especially helpful to discuss information with an instructor or another student.

Physiology can be a very demanding course; as with other first-year courses, the amount of material can be overwhelming. Be prepared to change gears when going from anatomy to physiology. Simple memorization will not be enough. This course requires an understanding of concepts and mechanisms and, more than any other medical school course, makes use of mathematical equations and calculations. If you are mathematically challenged, be forewarned.

Physiology involves many complex concepts and ideas. You may be frustrated if you don't understand the material after reviewing it once. That's perfectly normal. Many of these ideas can't be mastered in one session; it may take several trials to learn the material. Reviewing lectures with actual work problems is critical. They go hand-in-hand and the ability to successfully solve these problems demonstrates your mastery of the lecture material. Be careful to keep up with your studies since each lecture is built upon the one before. Falling behind can be disastrous.

For each topic in physiology, be sure you know the following:

- the overall function of the system being discussed

- key mathematical equations and formulas

- correlation with daily life phenomena (i.e., eating, exercise, breathing)

- correlation with clinical scenarios

- relationship with other physiological systems

Don't forget to bring your calculator to the exam. Physiology is your first medical school course that has clearly delineated clinical relevance. Knowledge you gain in this course will not only be very helpful in your third-year courses, but essential for the rest of your medical career.

Neuroscience

Neuroscience is the study of the brain and the rest of the nervous system. This is an interdisciplinary course, combining features of physiology and anatomy, along with a dash of histology and biochemistry. For example, the membrane potential and microscopic structure of the neuron are reintroduced in this course. You will study the function of chemical receptors in the brain, and the anatomy of the many cranial lobes that make up the brain.

Some students consider neuroscience the most fascinating course of the first year, as the brain is a unique organ with a vast array of functions, including all of the activities of daily living. Learning about the brain and the nervous system can be exciting as well as challenging. Since this course involves complex material taught in a short period of time, some students find it the most difficult course of the first year.

Lectures will stress the anatomy and physiology of the nervous system. Many different neural pathways and processes will be presented, and you'll be shown slides that illustrate the structure of the brain. These slides are extremely valuable. The brain is made of many components crammed into a small space; the visual representations on the slides make learning these structures a much less formidable task.

Just when you thought it was safe to put your dissection kit away, you'll be thrown back into the anatomy lab. This time, however, you won't have to worry about changing clothes or taking post-lab showers as the smell of formalin isn't as overwhelming. Equipment for this course is similar to that used in the anatomy lab: a dissection kit, a lab coat, an atlas, and a box of latex gloves.

Lab in this course is not as intense as it was in gross anatomy. You are dealing with only one organ and, in some schools, most of the dissection is done by the professor as many of the structures are small and delicate, requiring very intricate dissections. Once again, you'll find an atlas your most valuable tool.

Since neuroscience is an intense—and short—course, it's important to get organized early. You should approach studying neuroscience the same way you did anatomy. Memorization can't be avoided, but learning to correlate structure with function makes the job easier. The key, as always, is to keep on top of the material; you can't start learning the functions of the cranial nerves the day before the final exam. When studying, focus on the following:

- the function and pathway of the cranial nerves
- the name of each structure and its function in the brain
- the location of significant structures in the nervous system
- the pathways of specific cerebral and peripheral nervous tracts
- clinical correlations (i.e., a blow to the back of the head will affect a person's vision)
- correlations with daily life activities (i.e., reflexes, senses, motor activities)

There are many tools available to help you learn the structure of the nervous system. Other than the material from lab and lecture, you can utilize CT scans and MRIs, radiological images that give a three dimensional perspective of the brain. You can also use A.D.A.M.®, the interactive computer program that can serve as both an atlas and a dissector.

Exams consist of a written and a practical portion, testing both lab and lecture material. In the practical section, you will be asked to identify structures on a brain and/or on slides. The written part usually includes questions concerning structures, pathways, functions, and clinical correlations.

Neuroscience is an amazing subject, and you will have learned an incredible amount of material by the time the course is over. What makes this course even more special is the fact that, for the most part, the brain is still a medical mystery. Only a small portion of the human nervous system is understood. You will discover how exciting and unique this organ is, and appreciate how big a role it plays in the human body.

Behavioral Science

Behavioral science, which combines the study of medicine with the study of the social sciences and humanities, provides a needed change of pace. After spending most of the first year studying the "hard" sciences, you have the opportunity to experience the "human" side of medicine. For many students, this course serves as their first taste of clinical medicine.

Behavioral science is the study of normal and abnormal behavior; the purpose of this course is to broaden a student's awareness of important social issues affecting medicine today. This course is not as intense as your other basic science courses, but don't take it for granted. This is one of the few opportunities you'll have to learn in a more relaxed atmosphere.

Lectures cover a wide range of topics in both psychiatry and behavioral science, including important ethical and social issues such as abortion, doctcr-patient relationships, euthanasia, patient rights, family structure, and health care delivery. Additionally, topics concerning human behavior are emphasized, including life cycle, personality disorders, and sexuality.

Lecture material is supplemented by actual patient contact. You will have the opportunity to interview and interact with patients on a one-to-one basis, your first chance to begin to develop your interpersonal skills before your clinical years start. These skills are essential components to the practice of medicine; they will stay with you the rest of your medical career.

One student told us about his first patient encounter:

> I'll never forget the experience. I was the first in my group of seven students required to interview a patient. I was nervous. To make matters worse, the nurse had told us this particular patient was in isolation due to his contagious condition. This meant we had to wear masks and gowns. Dressed like an astronaut, I entered the room and introduced myself. The patient began screaming. Unbeknownst to me, this patient had a history of paranoid delusions. He thought the earth was being invaded by aliens, and he was the chosen subject for their experiments. The resident quickly escorted our group of aliens out of the room to avoid agitating the patient any further. To my disappointment, my first patient encounter was of the third kind.

Patient interviewing is a skill that takes many years to master. Treat the patient as you would a new acquaintance and remember that patients are usually as nervous as you are. If you are an outgoing person, then interacting with patients will be easier for you. If you are shy, then this initial contact will be more of a challenge. But with time and practice, you will feel more comfortable and assured.

Through this course, you will be introduced to the mental status exam. This provides a general description of a patient's manner and behavior. It includes an assessment of a person's:

- appearance: mannerisms, dress, etc.
- speech: coherence, flight of ideas, patterns, etc.
- mood and affect: emotion and responses
- thought process
- thought content
- motor activity
- cognitive functions: attention and concentration, memory, insight, and judgment

Since the concepts covered in behavioral science are straight-forward, studying is less of a chore than in your other courses. Additionally, this course is unique in that you have the ability to correlate lecture material with your own experiences, both personally and clinically, which makes studying much easier and more enjoyable. For example, you can relate the life cycle to your own experiences growing up. Or you may be able to correlate your studies of clinical depression with a patient you've seen. When studying you may want to place emphasis on the following:

- normal behavior and development
- behavioral and psychiatric disorders including: name, etiology, manifestation, and treatment
- important ethical issues in medicine (i.e., euthanasia, abortion, etc.)
- issues concerning doctor-patient relationships
- social issues (family structure, drug abuse, teenage preg-nancy, etc.)

Behavioral science also has many facts and statistics that need to be memorized and will be tested, such as: What percent of the population is elderly? What is the prevalence of eating disorders among college students? What age group most commonly abuses drugs? Behavioral science allows you to broaden your knowledge concerning the human side of medicine. In a complex health care system, it is easy to forget that being a doctor also means being a human being.

First Year Exams

Study Tips and Techniques

The medical school exam can get your adrenaline flowing like no exam has done before. Even if you are well-prepared, you can never completely escape stress and anxiety. This can be partially attributed to the fact that everybody else is nervous, and since this state of mind is often contagious, you will most likely find yourself feeling quite nervous as well. Acknowledging your exam anxieties to yourself is important, as it is possible for it to work in your favor. Anxiety produces adrenaline, which gives you the extra energy boost you need to get through the exam.

As you have probably gathered by now, the most important study tip is to do a moderate amount of studying each day so that it does not become an overwhelming task before each exam. Your note-taking, study sheets, and flash cards will have highlighted those areas that will be covered on the exam, and careful review of these study aids should allow you to absorb the important details without becoming immersed in minutiae.

It is your choice whether to study alone, with a study partner, or in a study group. For some students, studying with others offers a diversion from their own anxieties. Study groups allow for a relaxed time when members can test each other in a non-threatening and mutually supportive atmosphere; its success depends on your ability to find people whose personalities and study techniques are compatible with your own. If you find the presence of others to be too stressful for you, don't force yourself to join a group. There is no right or wrong way to study—only the way that works best for you.

Nutrition and sleep are more important to exam-taking than to any other brain function required during the preclinical years. Even though you may feel unprepared for an upcoming exam, don't give in to the temptation to pull an all-nighter. Psychological studies have shown that spaced repetitions produce twice the long-term memory retention that massed repetitions do. In other words, going over the material more than once, in study sessions that are spaced out in time and separated by other activities, produces greater retention of the material than trying to learn it all in one sitting.

If you think it might be useful to wake up super early in order to review your notes on an exam day, plan for this in advance and go to sleep early the night before. A good night's sleep helps you retain information and reduce anxiety.

Don't forget to give your brain the nourishment it requires. Mega-doses of multivitamins on the morning of the exam are not going to turn months of bad eating habits around for you on that day, but do eat a good breakfast. If you tend to get dehydrated, bring a bottle of water to the exam with you. If you tend to get hypoglycemic, bring along hard candies, a soft granola bar, or grapes.

Make sure that you are dressed comfortably for your exam, and that you have the necessary materials you may need. Bring a calculator if the material being tested involves mathematics problems. If you wear glasses, don't forget them, particularly if you need them for distance and part of the exam includes projected slides.

Finally, and perhaps most importantly, stay calm. Take deep breaths and relax. Clear your mind and focus. If you have studied the material, the answers will come to you. Nothing is worse than knowing that you know the answer but not being able to retrieve the information. The best technique for handling this situation is to sit back, close your eyes, and pretend that you are back in the library with your book open, reading about the topic in question. Perhaps you can picture the page in the book or the place on your study sheet where you recorded the answer.

This is what scientists call "state-bound knowledge." Every time we learn something new, it becomes "attached" to the state of consciousness in which we learned it. For example, if you learn someone's name at a party at which you had a particularly good time, that knowledge becomes attached to the state of consciousness you were in at the time of the party. If you want to recall that person's name, try to recreate the mood you were in at the party, and the name will come to you. Suppose you study for exams every day in your room with the sun streaming through the windows warming your back. When you actually take the exam, you will have a much easier time recalling the information you need if you can summon up the mood that you experienced in your room while studying, and the feeling of warmth on your back.

Although you may sometimes find it difficult to believe, course instructors want you to do well on their exams. After all, your performance is a reflection on how well they taught the course material, so naturally, they hope for good results. In addition, your medical school supports your doing well in class, and will likely respond to any concerns you may have about this process.

Competition and Grades

One doctor told us:

> *My first exam was in embryology. I thought I had done very well on it, somewhere in the 90s. They had put our grades in highest-to-lowest order, listed next to your social security number. I started at the top and kept looking for my number. By the time I found my 93, I saw that everyone else had done much better. At first, that was really hard to deal with. But as I went along I began to realize that there are plenty of students who do very well on tests from the beginning, but don't always go on to be good doctors—or to be doctors at all. And some students aren't good test-takers, but they have great rapport with their patients.*
>
> *I wish I'd known someone at the beginning who could have told me that it wasn't so important to be at the top of every single exam, that the reasons you wanted to become a doctor in the first place, and the qualities that helped you get into med school, are much more important than doing so well in the classroom.*

Most medical students are well acquainted with competition. Getting into medical school is, by its very nature, a highly competitive process. However, a delicate balance between competition and camaraderie among your classmates makes for the best learning environment as well as the most comfortable peer relationships.

There are two rules to follow which can help you tame the competitive monster:

Rule #1: Be Aware of Your Competitive Feelings

There is a difference between trying to do your best and trying to do better than everyone else. There's nothing wrong with setting high goals and working to achieve them, but strong competitive feelings often produce unnecessary stress and anxiety, and only get in the way of your success.

Rule #2: The Only Person You Have to Answer to is Yourself
Motivational speaker and success guru Earl Nightingale once defined success as "the progressive realization of a worthy goal." In other words, it's not where we finish, but how we get there that counts. Every time we take even the smallest step toward achieving a goal, we are successful. As a student working toward graduating from med school, you are not only successful on commencement day; you're successful every time you go to class, study, take a test, and learn something new. Your success has nothing to do with the fact that you may or may not get a better grade than others in your class.

Schools vary greatly in their competitive natures. Fifty percent of the students from Johns Hopkins University School of Medicine, for example, feel their classmates are extremely competitive, and most say they study very hard. Says one sophomore, "The coursework is not for the fainthearted. There is a lot of work required of everyone—even just to pass." The competition, heavy workload, and letter-grading system lead some to say that the school is "very stressful." On the opposite end, Yale University has a unique evaluation system in which there are no grades. This system produces an extremely non-competitive atmosphere. However, one student warns, "The amazing amount of latitude gives you the opportunity and time to pursue personal interests, but requires more self-discipline than might be needed at other, more regimented schools."

Regardless of your school's grading policies, your goal is to do your best. Most schools have a chapter of Alpha Omega Alpha, the national honor medical society, a somewhat mysterious organization, as each school has its own "formula" by which it chooses and inducts its members. AOA is not a requirement for reaching your residency goals, but it can be an impressive addition to your record.

Asking for Help and Finding a Tutor

It is not unusual to find your first year of medical school an intense and difficult experience. Many students discover themselves struggling through the strenuous academics, and some do not pass the final exams. For this reason, medical schools offer tutors to aid in learning the material and adopting more effective study skills. Although you may have reservations about accepting help, allowing yourself to take advantage of this service will inevitably pay off in the long run.

How do you know when it is time to be concerned enough to get help? Sometimes your school may pick this up before you do, and your Dean of Students may ask to meet with you. If this does not happen, but you are concerned about your own performance, you are welcome to arrange an appointment with the Dean on your own. This office will connect you with an appropriate person or give you the name of someone who can help you in a particular course. Your medical school wants you to succeed in reaching your goals; you would not have been accepted for admission if the school did not feel you have what it takes to do well. For many, the individual attention and support of a tutor is enough to get them back on track.

If you feel that the extra help is not sufficient and you continue to struggle without successfully passing the courses, it might be worth repeating a year or slowing down and lightening your course load, thereby extending your first two years into three or more. This is not an unusual course of action, particularly for people who have additional stresses in their lives, such as illness or family responsibilities. Once again, the Dean of Students will be happy to help you arrange a schedule that will allow you to reach your goal of becoming a doctor.

SUMMER!

The good news is: you've survived your first year of medical school! Most students are relieved to finish what is invariably considered a tough year emotionally and physically. Now that the academic year is completed, it is time to think about your summer plans. The bad news is that the summer between first and second year is your last "free" summer during medical school. Depending on your school, you will have two to three months of vacation.

Make the most of this free time; you may not have it again for several years. Summer usually means one of three things: an opportunity to take a vacation, a chance to do research, or a chance to work and earn some extra money. The choice is entirely yours.

Since you have been sitting in lecture halls and classrooms for the past year, you may require the summer off to recuperate and recharge your batteries. This may also be your last chance to paddle down the Amazon River or to climb Mt. Everest for a long time to come.

Research in the clinical or basic sciences is another option; it gives you a chance to explore new avenues in medicine to which you might not otherwise be exposed, and you may discover what fields of medicine interest you most. It could also pay financially and enhance your resume. Residency programs often look favorably on applicants who have research experience. Speak to your mentor or visit the student affairs office; they will have a list of research opportunities.

Your third option is to use this time to earn money to help offset some of your medical school expenses. Again, the student affairs office may be able to help you secure summer employment.

Gear your summer to your specific needs and career plans. Whether you just want to relax on the beach or work in the immunology lab, there is no right or wrong decision. And you are not limited to one choice. You might choose a combination of the three options, taking a few weeks for vacation and spending the rest of the summer earning money as a lab assistant. No matter what you decide, make the best use of your last free summer. Enjoy yourself.

CHAPTER 4

The Second Year

WHAT YOU CAN EXPECT

The second year concludes your journey through the basic sciences. Second year is taught much the same way as first year, using lectures, labs, and small group discussions. The main difference is that you get greater exposure to the hospital setting. Material taught during this year will be more pertinent to what a clinician really needs to know. Furthermore, you will actually be able to answer many of the medical questions thrown your way by your grandmother and her friends.

Courses covered during the second year include pathology/pathophysiology, microbiology, pharmacology, and introduction to clinical medical/physical diagnosis. The advantage you have during the second year is that you can call upon the study and test-taking techniques you developed during the first year. You already know what works for you and what doesn't. You have made friends and established study groups.

Most students are glad to get to the second year. It brings you much closer to what we typically think of as being a doctor. Second-year classes are concerned with teaching you to understand, diagnose, and treat diseases. During this year, you will interact with patients. Some schools introduce patient contact in the first year. If this is so in your school, the amount of patient contact will increase.

Keep in mind that being a second-year student does not mean you can forget all the information you learned during your first year. Each course and each year builds on the ones before it, and represents a step in your development as a physician. And at the end of the second year, you take Step 1 of the National Boards, which tests all the material from the first two years.

SECOND YEAR COURSES

Pathology/Pathophysiology

Pathology is the course that links the basic sciences with clinical medicine. Material learned from anatomy, histology, physiology, biochemistry, and neuroscience is always referred to in pathology. The focus of this subject is disease processes. Pathology is defined as the science or the study of the origin, nature, and course of diseases. Unlike first year courses that dealt with normal states, pathology deals more with abnormal states. Concrete information relating to patient care is emphasized.

Pathology is concerned with all aspects of disease, its causes, and the development of abnormal conditions. Because of the extensive amount of material involved, this is a year-long course. This amount of time is necessary to learn all of pathology. After all, the study of disease processes is the cornerstone of all clinical medicine.

In your pathology course, some of the subjects you will study include heart disease, blood vessel diseases, immunology, infectious diseases, respiratory system diseases, and environmentally induced diseases. You'll also cover organ systems including the liver, pancreas, and kidney, the urinary and gastrointestinal tracts, the skin, breasts and genitals, the spleen, the nervous system, and the musculoskeletal system.

Teaching in pathology is done through the use of lectures, labs, and small group discussions. The best aspect of pathology is that lectures are taught by clinical practitioners. For this reason, lectures give you a sense of what being a physician really means. Topics are broken down by system, the same way physiology and anatomy were. For each system covered, the corresponding disease processes and abnormal states are discussed. Lectures will emphasize the incidence, the etiology, and the clinical course of each disease. The anatomical changes and structural manifestations caused by each disease are also discussed. All this information is essential to clinicians in the diagnosis and treatment of their patients.

Slides are an integral part of lectures. They show the gross and microscopic changes in anatomy that result from disease processes. You may first want to review your atlases from anatomy and histology. Keep in mind that you need to know both normal anatomy and structure before you attempt to master abnormal conditions. Being able to visualize physical changes while learning about disease states makes the material easier to grasp.

Studying pathology means it is time to dig out the microscope again. Lab focuses on visualizing both microscopic slides and gross specimens. You will be examining slides showing the microscopic changes caused by disease processes. The key here is to be able to recognize a normal specimen, because once you are able to do that, you can learn to identify diseased tissue. By distinguishing the differences, you can formulate a list of possible diseases. From this list, a diagnosis can be obtained.

In addition to microscopic slides, you will be presented with kodachromes and gross specimens showing different disease processes. Once again, the ability to distinguish normal from diseased conditions will put you one step ahead of the game. If you find that you can't identify a sample, you can always ask your professor or look in an atlas.

Difficulties can arise in learning to recognize the gross and microscopic changes in disease processes. Do the following to help yourself in lab:

- spend time examining slides, kodachromes, and gross specimens

- compare each specimen with an example of a normal state, focusing on specific differences

- practice identifying unknown slides and specimens

- ask questions when something is not clear to you

During pathology, most schools require their students to attend an autopsy. This is a postmortem examination of the human body. Pathologists sometimes use this exam to help them determine the cause of death and to study any abnormal anatomical changes. Attending an autopsy ties material from lab and lecture with actual clinical medicine.

A group of students visits a hospital morgue to observe and participate in an actual autopsy. The morgue is exactly the way you imagine it will be. The room contains several autopsy tables, some occupied, others empty. It is cold and windowless. The air is stagnant. Don't be surprised if you have a "lethal" reaction to your first autopsy. In fact, by the time the autopsy is over, many students look and feel like they belong on one of the empty procedure tables.

In an autopsy, pathologists make incisions in the body to expose the individual organs. Each organ is measured, weighed, and examined for any anatomical changes or defects. From this information, a differential diagnosis can be inferred. The differential diagnosis is further scrutinized and incorporated into the particular patient's clinical picture in determining the cause of death.

You think you're prepared for an autopsy because you've dissected a cadaver. But you get to an autopsy within twenty-four hours of death, so you're dealing with a warm body. It bleeds. It's scary, but it's fascinating as well.
Medical student, Columbia University College of Physicians and Surgeons

---

In the small, group problem-solving sessions, you will have a chance to review clinical cases, clarify unclear material, and ask questions relevant to the topics covered in lecture. Here you will discuss the cause of the disease, the diagnosis, the relevant structural changes, and finally, the treatment. These clinical scenarios may seem difficult at first, but with time you will become more skilled at solving these cases. This skill will not only reinforce your knowledge of the material, but will be crucial to you in your clinical years.

Learning the language and concepts behind pathology can make this course a difficult one to master. Not only must you keep up with the material, but you may need to read ahead to understand the topics as they are presented to you. Just as in the first year, incorporating lab and lecture with the problem-solving sessions will give you a better grasp of the material. Focus your studying to include:

- the comprehension of normal processes and structures (anatomy, histology, physiology, etc.)

- learning the major diseases of each organ system

- knowing the incidence, etiology, and mechanism of each disease

- the correlation of the disease with the slides, kodachromes, or gross specimens showing anatomical changes

- the clinical significance and manifestations of each disease

- incorporating examples from your autopsy session and problem-solving sessions with your studying

There is one thing to watch out for during the study of pathology. You suddenly notice aches and pains you had previously ignored. Mosquito bites turn into malaria. Indigestion is a sure sign of an ulcer. You begin to believe that every small symptom you experience represents a fatal disease. The more you read about each disease, the more you become convinced you have a major case of it. There is, however, no need to worry. You don't have a fatal illness. What you do have is a common affliction known as the "Medical Student Syndrome."

Every student goes through this at one time or another. When learning cardiac pathology, for example, you may think you have a fatal cardiac arrhythmia every time your heart rate increases. Splitting headaches, you may believe, represent brain tumors. And, although you're positive that your upset stomach is caused by some obscure tropical parasite, it's once again the medical student syndrome—a transient, non-fatal, normal reaction. When you make it through the year without actually contracting any of these exotic illnesses, you'll know that you've finally come to your senses.

Pathology exams cover material from lecture, lab and problem-solving sessions. The written portion is a free-for-all that can include any and all of the material covered during the year. You have to know pathological processes, clinical correlations, and pathophysiology. The practical portion involves identifying unknown slides or kodachromes and incorporating them with clinical topics. As you look at an unknown slide, try first to identify the tissue type. Next, determine the problem. Finally, correlate this information with a specific disease process.

Without question, pathology is a tough course. It requires many hours of study, but the rewards are great. The value of a strong working knowledge of disease processes will become apparent in the first few minutes of the National Boards, and more importantly, on the first day of your clinical rotations.

Microbiology

Microbiology is the science or study of the structure, function, and uses of microscopic organisms. Since the beginning of time, man has been combating diseases caused by microorganisms. Infectious disease is one of the most common problems afflicting patients in hospitals today. Microbiology offers the student insight into the worlds of bacteria and viruses. This course emphasizes the effect of these microorganisms on people's health.

Microbiology is one of the more important subjects, not only for your clinical rotations, but for the National Boards as well. The course itself is straightforward, without many difficult concepts to master. The main objective is to build a fundamental knowledge of the "world of bugs." This world involves a new language and ideas unrelated to any previous medical school courses.

While microbiology deals with the study of bacteria, viruses, and other microorganisms, immunology is a subsection of microbiology concerned with the body's defenses against infection. Through lectures and labs, topics in both microbiology and immunology are discussed. Through the use of clinical correlations, you will learn the theories necessary to diagnose, treat, and prevent infectious disease.

Instructors will discuss different types of microorganisms including bacteria, fungi, and the hundreds of parasites that can infect human beings. You'll be taught about viruses in their many forms, and how they reproduce, infect, and transmit a range of illnesses from the common cold to AIDS. Topics covered will highlight microorganisms and their properties, their effect on the human host, and the antibiotics and chemotherapeutic agents used to treat them. In addition, the role of the immune system's response to these infectious agents will be stressed. The significance of this becomes obvious when discussing diseases such as AIDS, tuberculosis, and chicken pox.

In lab, you will work in a group. Lab sessions will focus on identifying organisms, growing cultures, and testing antibiotics. You will need a microscope and an atlas to help you in this identification process. Important techniques taught include culture inoculation and Gram staining (a method of staining and distinguishing bacteria using crystal violet). If you are an artist, you'll enjoy microbiology. Gram staining and other procedures using dyes and inks can be quite creative—and messy. One medical student who was a former artist, for example, made tie-dyed tee shirts every time he prepared a Gram stain. His lab partners spent the year debating whether or not this was intentional.

As in any new procedure, the more you practice, the more proficient you will become. These skills will be utilized in the hospital setting. For example, throat cultures are used in the diagnosis of strep throat.

The strength of microbiology is the laboratory work. Much of the material in this course can be dry and tedious. In lab, however, you have the opportunity to make the course more interesting and fun. You will have a chance to grow microorganisms in the lab and thus observe their individual properties and characteristics. For example, you will discover that fungi emit a unique and unforgettable odor. Some bacteria may produce colorful colonies or grow in interesting patterns. Other bacteria require special growth mediums, like chocolate agar. The following hints may help you in laboratory:

- Be organized.

- Prepare your materials ahead of time. This is especially important for Gram staining and inoculations.

- Label—and include your name—on everything before you begin work.

- Familiarize yourself with pictures of organisms in the atlas.

- When identifying unknowns, use flow charts to keep track of the different characteristics for each organism. This will make it easier to make an identification.

- Never hesitate to ask questions in lab when something is unclear.

Memorization may be the best study strategy for this course. You want to develop a good knowledge of the major "bugs" and their general characteristics. A good way to organize this material is to use index cards. Each card should contain one organism. For each organism, you can list its shape, growth requirements (medium), mechanism of infection, and disease state. In addition, you may wish to add methods of diagnosis and treatment. If index cards are not your style, charts are a useful alternative.

Do the following to help you organize your studying:

- learn the name of the organism and its general characteristics
- understand the organism's method of infection
- relate the organism with the clinical manifestations and treatment
- learn the body's mechanism of defense against each organism
- know the geographic distribution of an organism and its related disease
- compare and contrast the above with other organisms

Integrating material from lecture and lab allows you to correlate the clinical diagnosis and treatment of infectious diseases. This is useful in preparing for exams. Exams and practicals usually emphasize this correlation.

Microbiology is an exciting subject. With all the new research being done in infectious disease and immunology, this field is at the forefront of medicine. Every day, new organisms and new treatment modalities are being discovered. Equipped with a good working knowledge of microbiology, you will be well prepared to tackle the years of clinical medicine that lay ahead of you.

Pharmacology

Pharmacology is the science dealing with the preparation, uses, and especially the effects of drugs. Medications are the most commonly used treatment today. For almost every disease, there is a corresponding drug used in its treatment. Physicians, as a result, must therefore be concerned with the effects individual drugs have on the patients they treat.

Making sense of pharmacology requires knowledge of physiology, anatomy, biochemistry, and neuroscience. These are courses you've taken before. If you feel you've forgotten some of the old material, it is critical to review it beforehand. Pharmacology will become more meaningful to you if you consolidate it with the previously studied course material.

The science of pharmacology explores the therapeutic and adverse effects of medication on patients. Through lectures and demonstrations, topics dealing with the mechanisms of drug action will be discussed. This will be correlated with clinical applications, thereby enhancing your understanding of the practical aspects of drug use. Without question, this is valuable information every doctor needs to know.

The course covers many different classes of drugs. These medications are grouped together either by the organ system they effect, by drug type, or by mechanism of action. Lecturers focus on drug names, mechanisms of action, side effects, drug interactions, and pharmacokinetics (the properties of drugs within the body). You'll learn, for example, that Albuterol is an asthma medication that works by relaxing airway smooth muscle.

Lectures are correlated with demonstrations showing the effects of drugs on animals. For example, rabbits are sometimes used to show the cardiovascular effects of certain medications. After administering epinephrine to the rabbit, changes in blood pressure, pulse, and heart rate are noted, an effective way of demonstrating the clinical effects of medication.

Studying pharmacology is once again like learning a new language. You have to memorize a basic vocabulary of the names and functions of medications used in clinical practice. It is important to understand the reasoning behind prescribing a particular drug. Don't spend time memorizing drug dosages, however. At this stage, it is neither emphasized nor important.

Memorizing information about drugs can be time-consuming. A basic strategy is therefore necessary to make your studying more manageable. The key is to make certain you understand the mechanisms by which a drug works. Again, organization is crucial. Index cards and charts can come to your rescue again. Each card or chart should contain one drug. For each of these drugs, you can list its formula, mechanism of action, clinical use, side effects, and interactions with other medications. You can do this for each class of drugs as you learn them. Other basic concepts stressed include:

- understanding the structural and functional bases of drug actions

- selecting representative drugs in each class and learning them thoroughly (properties, clinical relevance, etc.)

- noting differences among the representative drug and two or three other drugs in that class

- relating personal experience with medications to your studies (i.e., medications for allergies, asthma and hypertension)

By getting organized early, you will be better prepared come exam time. The National Boards often present problems correlating pharmacology with clinical examples. Make sure you understand the clinical relevance of each drug.

Pharmacology is a challenging course. Nevertheless, you'll learn to master a skill that is essential to the practice of medicine. There are an endless number of drugs flooding the marketplace today, and new discoveries are being made each week. Every doctor needs to know how to effectively prescribe the right drugs for each patient. The basic knowledge you gain in this course will serve as the foundation of the pharmaceutical choices you will have to make throughout your medical career.

Clinical Medicine/Physical Diagnosis

Welcome to clinical skills. Finally, you leave the classroom and enter the hospital. Physical diagnosis is a practical course. Your time is spent getting direct bedside experience in evaluating patients. For many students, this is the first time they get to do a complete examination on a patient. Clinical skills provide the transition between the basic and clinical sciences.

You may feel apprehensive when you are beginning physical diagnosis. You might not think you're ready to play doctor yet. Relax. Every great doctor had to begin somewhere.

In this course, you will be expected to perform a complete history and physical exam. The information that you learned in your year of study will play a vital role in clinical problem-solving. Your goal for this course is to fine-tune your observation and examination skills.

Although the focus of the course is on direct patient interaction, lectures and demonstrations are used to teach the procedures for taking a history and performing a physical examination. Demonstrations will be conducted using real patients or student volunteers. As each of the organ systems is discussed, you will learn to master specific diagnostic techniques. For example, when you listen to the heart, you'll know how to position the patient in various ways to elicit specific heart sounds.

Before you start, you will need to buy some medical equipment. Depending on your school, you will either buy your equipment through a distributor, or purchase it on your own. It is usually less expensive to purchase your equipment through a school-supported distributor because they sell in bulk. Essential equipment includes a stethoscope, a short white coat, a pen light, a tuning fork, and a reflex hammer. If you really want to go overboard, you can also purchase an opthalmoscope (an instrument for viewing the interior of the eye) an otoscope (an instrument for examining the external canal and tympanic membrane of the ear), a blood pressure cuff, surgical scissors, and a year's supply of suture material. This equipment is not necessary, and can usually be found at the hospital. However, if you want to own this equipment, you might try looking for a relative who is excited enough about your becoming a doctor to foot the bill.

Since you will be working in a hospital and dealing with patients, you should dress in a neat, professional manner. That means a dress shirt, slacks, tie, and shoes for men, and a nice blouse with slacks, a skirt or a dress, and shoes for women. Don't wear jeans or sneakers. Remember, you're a physician in training now. You must not only act the part, but dress the part as well.

When dealing with patients, you want to present yourself as professionally as possible. Be courteous, friendly, and most of all, respectful of their privacy. Before beginning an examination, introduce yourself. When talking with them, make eye contact and smile. It doesn't cost you anything and your return will be immense. As you interview more patients, you will begin to develop your own style. In the meantime, enjoy yourself and try to learn as much as you can.

For many students, one of the more awkward experiences is examining a patient of the opposite sex. To prepare you for this, some schools offer instruction prior to entering the hospital. This often involves performing a complete gynecological exam using surrogate patients to instruct students in performing a breast and pelvic exam. You may feel anxious. However, this is a practice session where mistakes are not counted against you. The surrogate patients are well-trained volunteers who are interested in teaching students. They serve to help you become more confident and more skillful in performing your gynecological exams.

You will also perform a complete genital and prostate exam on male patients. Although schools have not yet adopted a formal surrogate patient program for this, the skill is taught during physical diagnosis. You can practice on patients in the hospital. Your instructor will guide you through the proper techniques for performing this exam.

The following is a list of helpful diagnostic hints. For each of the organ systems discussed, make sure you understand:

- the basic anatomy and physiology
- how to take an appropriate history by asking relevant questions
- the specific signs and symptoms
- the basic procedures of the physical exam (including inspection, palpation (touch), percussion (striking or tapping), and auscultation (listening, either directly or through a stethoscope)
- clinical correlations

When interviewing and examining patients, you should:

- **Always be courteous and respectful**.
- Always introduce yourself when first meeting the patient.
- Listen to what your patient says.
- Always tell the patient what you're going to do before you actually do it.
- Remember it is the patient's body you're examining. He or she has a right to refuse any part of the physical examination.
- Never discuss patient conditions in a public place. This information is confidential.

Clinical skills introduces you to the art and basic techniques of examining a patient. Each student is expected to learn how to take a complete, relevant medical history, perform a complete physical examination, begin to recognize both normal and abnormal findings and to present the clinical findings in a concise and informative fashion. Mastering the physical diagnosis is the first real step in patient care. The treatment of a patient always begins with a history and physical. No diagnosis can be made without this.

> *It was the day of my final exam in physical diagnosis. My preceptor and I were wandering the hospital in search of a patient to examine. After several unsuccessful tries, we finally came upon an elderly lady. The preceptor began asking the patient some questions to make sure she was a suitable candidate. She did not reply. The preceptor asked the same questions again, this time in a louder voice. Again, the patient did not respond. Puzzled, I looked around for an answer. Above her head hung a large sign which stated, "Patient is a deaf mute." I pointed this out to my preceptor. He was embarrassed to realize he had failed his own exam. The first rule of physical diagnosis, the power of observation, had been overlooked. It's a lesson that I'm sure neither of us will ever forget.*
>
> **Resident, Sloan Kettering Memorial Hospital**

Electives

During the basic science years, you may have elective courses as part of your curriculum. Depending on the school, your choices will vary. Since schools offer such a wide variety of elective choices, an attempt to mention them all would be beyond the scope of this book. For example, courses are offered in the history of medicine, medical ethics, substance abuse, primary care, and empathy training, just to mention a few.

One associate professor of an upstate New York medical center told us:

I teach a course called "The Anatomy of the Health Care System." Students follow the progress of a patient who has to go through the system with a chronic illness. In our case, it's asthma. The students have to try and negotiate the system from the patient's point of view. Another course I teach is in medical reasoning skills. That involves learning to read medical literature intelligently and critically, learning how to evaluate studies for their strengths and weaknesses, and how to apply this information to clinical decision making.

One elective that is standard for most schools is community and preventive medicine. This is a course dealing with important health care issues and other information not usually covered in the basic science curriculum. Material discussed includes biostatistics, epidemiology (the study of epidemic diseases), preventive medicine, and public health issues. Emphasis is placed on the student developing an awareness of these important issues and clinical problem solving. Knowledge gained from this course can then be readily applied to other medical school courses, to research, and to any medical field entered. Community and preventive medicine is an important course; material covered in it appears on the National Boards.

NATIONAL BOARDS PART I

During your first two years in medical school, this is the test professors are constantly talking about. Many professors teach for the Boards: "This will be covered on the Boards"; "You need to know this for the Boards"; "Don't worry about that, it won't be on the Boards...."

What are the Boards, and who gives them? The United States Medical Licensing Examination (USMLE), a.k.a., the Boards, is a test made up of three steps that evaluate applicants for medical licensure in the United States. The USMLE is a joint program of the Federation of State Medical Boards of the United States, Inc., and the National Board of Medical Examiners.

The USMLE is designed to assess a physician's ability to apply the knowledge, concepts, and principles important to health and disease that constitute the basis for safe and effective patient care. Each step of the USMLE is taken independently and is complementary to the others. No step can stand alone in the assessment process for medical licensure. Each step requires two days of testing. In order to move to the next step, you must pass the step before it. Unlike the MCAT exams, once a step is passed it cannot be retaken, except in cases of failure. In other words, you cannot take it again to get a higher grade.

Each part is administered twice a year. Step 1 is given in both June and September following the completion of the second year of medical school. Step 1 covers the material from the first two years of study (basic sciences). This exam assesses a student's ability to apply his or her knowledge and understanding of key biomedical science concepts. The emphasis is on the principles and mechanisms of health, disease, and treatment modalities.

The National Boards is a minimum competency exam. The significance of this should not be overlooked. Traditionally, medical schools required students to take the exams, but did not demand that they pass them in order to graduate. As time goes by, however, more and more medical schools are requiring that students pass these exams in order to continue on to the third year.

Schools use these tests as an external measure of a student's cognitive competence. This allows them to compare students from different schools on an equivalent basis. In addition, schools use this test for their self-assessment, as a measure of their teaching effectiveness. Internship and residency committees also use these scores in evaluating their applicants. Depending on the specialty, Board scores may or may not play an important role in postgraduate training selection. Make it your job to find out ahead of time if your desired specialty uses Board scores as a criterion for acceptance.

USMLE Step 1 is a two-day, twelve-hour exam. Each day consists of two three-hour sections, separated by a lunch break. The exam consists of multiple-choice and matching questions. Each test section covers all subject material. Questions are dispersed across all topic areas. Some test questions are accompanied by pictures, graphs, and tables, which students are asked to interpret or identify. Pictures are of both gross and microscopic normal and pathologic specimens. Other questions test basic knowledge and the student's ability to apply basic science material to clinical scenarios.

Topics covered on USMLE Step 1 include:

- Anatomy
- Behavioral Sciences
- Biochemistry
- Microbiology
- Pathology
- Physiology
- Pharmacology
- Aging
- Nutrition
- Genetics

Questions are broken down by:

1. System
   a. General principles
   b. Individual organ systems
      1. Cardiovascular
      2. Hematopoietic/Lymphoreticular
      3. Gastrointestinal
      4. Nervous/Special Senses
      5. Renal/Urinary
      6. Skin/Connective Tissue
      7. Reproductive
      8. Musculoskeletal
      9. Endocrine
      10. Pulmonary/Respiratory
2. Process
   a. Normal
   b. Abnormal
3. Organizational level
   a. Person/Group
   b. Multilevel
   c. Organ/Tissue
   d. Cells/Subcellular
   e. Molecular
   f. Nonhuman organism
   g. Exogenous substances

Test results are usually mailed to you six to eight weeks after the exam date. After opening the envelope, you will see two numbers. One, a two-digit number, represents a percentile score. The other, a three-digit number, represents a raw score. Raw scores will range between 140 and 260. The mean is 200, and the minimum passing score is 176. This is converted to a two-digit percentile with 82 representing the mean, and 75 representing the minimum passing score. The minimum passing score usually translates into answering between 55 and 65 percent of the questions correctly. You can find more information about the National Boards in chapter 9.

Half of your medical school career is now over. By this time, you should feel closer to becoming a doctor. These two years of basic science have equipped you with the language and vocabulary necessary to venture forth into the world of clinical medicine. This is the strong foundation on which you will build your success in your last two years of school.

CHAPTER 5

Transition from the Classroom to the Hospital

What You Can Expect

Congratulations! You are now halfway through your medical school education. You have survived the pressures of the first two years and taken the first and most difficult part of the National Boards. You're now ready to make the transition from the classroom, where you spent most of the last two years, to the hospital ward, where you will spend most of the next two years.

This will be a fascinating and exciting time, but will also be filled with nerve-racking experiences, from finding your way around to understanding your role with your colleagues and with your patients. Each day of the next two years will expose you to new situations and present you with new information.

In the third year of medical school you'll be participating in five two-to-three-month rotations (also known as clerkships) in internal medicine, general surgery, obstetrics/gynecology (OB-GYN), pediatrics, and psychiatry. The remaining two months will be spent on electives and vacation time. You will most likely settle your schedule of rotations during your second year. Medical schools vary greatly regarding flexibility and which rotations must be completed during which year. The bottom line is that everybody completes every rotation at one time or another, so when you schedule each rotation is more or less a matter of personal preference.

The various rotations serve as introductions to the five main areas of medical practice. Their primary function is to help you decide which area you would like to pursue after graduation. Some students know their field of interest even before they apply to medical school; others don't make this decision until after they've completed all their rotations.

One medical student who thought that she was interested in surgery decided that she wanted to do her surgical rotation early in the year in order to confirm this interest and then be able to compare her experience in surgery to her other rotations. This turned out to be a good decision, as she discovered that she did not want to go into surgery after all, and was then able to face her other rotations with a completely open mind.

Another student felt that he would most likely choose a residency in internal medicine, but he was concerned about his ability to do the many procedures, or "scut work," expected of the medical student in the hospital. Because he wanted to be less nervous about his procedural skills and more focused on learning during his internal medicine rotation, he chose to start his third year with his OB-GYN clerkship. He knew that there he would have the opportunity to learn to draw blood and put in IVs on young, healthy, pregnant patients with very large veins secondary to their increased blood volume. By the time his rotation in internal medicine came up a few months later, he was able to perform basic procedures with ease and was given the opportunity to try some more advanced procedures under the supervision of the resident on his team.

A third student knew that she was going to have to decide between her interests in pediatrics and psychiatry. She chose to start her year with her internal medicine rotation, figuring that this would give her a solid basis and expose her to many different kinds of patients, allowing her a sense of general confidence about her role in the wards. She elected to do both pediatrics and psychiatry in the middle of the year. That gave her time at the end of the year to decide which electives she would take as a fourth year student and make her decision about which residency she would apply for.

COMING TO THE HOSPITAL

Your Attire

In the last chapter, we talked about proper attire for your time at the hospital; part of that attire is the short white coat you are expected to wear whenever you're on duty (however, you may not be expected to wear this coat while you're doing your pediatrics or psychiatry rotations). Although some medical students find the white coat to be annoying, it serves many purposes. It can help you keep warm in the normally chilly hospital. Its many pockets allow you to carry instruments, pocket-size books, and note cards with key facts and patient information. Your white coat also identifies you as a physician to the patients, which is an important part of developing a relationship with them. Make sure you have some identification visible on your outfit, such as your hospital ID card or a name tag, at least one of which is normally required by the hospital.

What you bring with you to the hospital varies depending on which rotation you are doing, and whether or not certain equipment is already provided. You have probably already purchased most of the basic medical equipment for your physical diagnosis course, and now you need to sift through it to be sure you are not missing anything important. You will be expected to have a stethoscope always available, and you need it often enough that you may as well just hang it around your neck. Be sure to label this and any other expensive equipment with your name and where you can be reached; a patient ID bracelet can be handy for this purpose.

Important items to keep in your pockets include a small working flashlight, a reflex hammer, and a small, lightweight ruler. Be sure to have at least two pens with black ink, one for writing notes and the other as backup when you misplace the first. Also be sure to have small file cards or a small spiral bound pad that you can quickly pull out to jot down notes.

Your Role on the Treatment Team

Although it may not always seem so to the patient or the visitor, a hospital is more than a gaggle of white-coated individuals running around healing the sick. It is actually run by well-coordinated teams of health-care professionals, each with a particular role to fill. As a medical student, you have a definite place on that team. You are still a student, which means that there are limits to your functions and responsibilities on the team, but your contributions to the team are vitally important and should be taken seriously. However, your main responsibility as a medical student is to learn as much as you can by observing the experienced professionals around you.

Once you understand the hierarchical system of the treatment team and where you fit into this system, you should feel completely comfortable in your role as a medical student. It can be frustrating, feeling that you are low person on the totem pole. However, as you get further into the third year rotations, you will appreciate the sense of protection you get from the people ahead of you who have to make the real decisions.

One of the most important decisions you can make to assure success in your third year is to put away your ego while you're working. Getting along with the people on your medical team is part of being a good medical student. Remember, you need these people on your side. Not only do they contribute to your evaluations, they are the people who will teach you some of the most important concepts in medicine.

Among the members of the treatment team, the intern is the most recent graduate from medical school, often the hardest working, and always the lowest paid. Although only two years ahead of you, your intern may have a ton to teach you, and the least amount of time to do so. When given the opportunity, tag along with the intern. That way you are able to see a lot of patients, perhaps help with or actually perform a number of procedures, and begin to apply your book learning to real life clinical situations.

The resident on the team to which you have been assigned has the greatest responsibility for teaching the medical students. This is not classroom-style teaching, but on-the-job training. If time allows, you can ask your resident to sit down with you or with a group of students to review specific concepts or general topics. But most of the time, you will learn by watching your resident in action, and by participating in various procedures.

An attending physician is always available to the treatment team, and, depending on the specialty and the specifics of the service, is involved in direct decision-making about patient care. Different attendings take on varying degrees of interest in the medical students on the team, usually based on how much time they have available, and how much teaching responsibility is expected of them by the clerkship director. If the attending is not available for a lot of teaching, observe and absorb information through the interactions of the attending and the residents (also called the housestaff).

Other members of the treatment team with whom you will have frequent contact are the nurses and other hospital ward staff, including social workers, nurses' aids, ward clerks, ancillary staff including phlebotomists and technologists, and other hospital administrators. Although your jobs may all seem extremely different, you are all members of the treatment team and all have the interest of the patient in mind. For this reason, it is useful to develop good professional relationships with other treatment team members, respecting the various disciplines and responsibilities of each.

Finally, you will be working closely with your fellow medical students, often on the same teams, while you are doing the same rotations. Competitive feelings can be intense during this period, when everyone is trying to impress the residents and attendings. However, your ability to work as part of a team is also being evaluated, so it is in your own best interest to curb those feelings and concentrate on doing your job.

One fourth-year medical student told us about her surgery rotation during her third year of medical school:

> I remember getting so frustrated when the clerkship director would go around the room quizzing each of us on a particular topic which we had just reviewed. Bob, another third year student, would loudly whisper the answers during everybody else's turn. I wanted to announce that he was disturbing me and not giving me a fair chance to answer the questions, but I was afraid of appearing argumentative and petty. Soon enough, the clerkship director interrupted the session and asked Bob to stop his inappropriate behavior. Bob's competitive nature got him in trouble. And I learned that keeping my competitive urges to myself paid off in the end.

The ideal is for everyone on the team to be respected for his or her contribution and treated fairly by every other member of the team, but in some unfortunate situations, medical students are treated in an inappropriate manner by the attending physician or housestaff. If you feel that any type of abuse or sexual harassment is taking place, consider speaking to the director of your clerkship or to the Dean Of Medical Students. Take your concerns seriously, not just for your sake, but for the sake of your fellow medical students as well.

Your Role with the Patient

A unique aspect of the job of clinical clerk, or medical student, on the hospital ward is the amount of time you get to spend with your patients. This time decreases as you become busier and busier over the course of your training, so take advantage of this special opportunity to practice forming relationships with your patients. You will learn a tremendous amount about the nature of doctor-patient and doctor-family relationships, knowledge that will serve you well in the future.

Nevertheless, it is crucial to recognize the limitations of your responsibility within the domain of patient care. Certainly, any concerns you may have about information that the patient has told you, or a physical exam finding you believe you have identified, deserve to be passed on to your intern or resident. Don't take it upon yourself to keep a patient's secret. If a patient wants to share something with you in confidence, explain that you must share the information with the other doctors if you consider this necessary. Don't feel shy about mentioning a concern you may have to your intern or resident. No matter how silly you think the information may be, it could be crucial to the patient's care and treatment. You need to be sure that you protect yourself and your patient; taking on inappropriate responsibility may be tempting but it is clearly in violation of your patient's well-being.

One medical student remembers her first patient while on rotation on a general medicine unit:

> *Mr. C was a 60-year-old postal worker who had been admitted for congestive heart failure. Each morning I would check his heart and breath sounds to follow his progress on newly prescribed medications. One morning, Mr. C looked less comfortable than usual and complained of intense left leg and foot pain. As he had been mostly sedentary during his hospital stay, I first thought of the possibility that Mr. C had developed at DVT, or deep vein thrombosis. I remembered learning about the "Homan's sign" in physical diagnosis, a benign procedure whereby if I flexed Mr. C's left ankle with my hands, he would experience*

extreme discomfort. I performed this maneuver, and Mr. C practically jumped out of his bed in pain. I ran to the nurse's station to find my intern and inform her of this serious finding.

On morning rounds, the team seemed particularly impressed by my knowledge and discovery of the DVT. The attending physician then went in to examine Mr. C and identified the early signs of gout in Mr. C's toes and ankle, a disorder leading to intense tenderness in the affected joints—joints that I had eagerly manipulated earlier that morning. Luckily for Mr. C, the diagnosis was less serious and more easily treatable than mine, and I learned an important lesson from my hasty assumptions.

One aspect of working with patients that you never become comfortable with is dealing with death. As time goes on, however, you will be able to distance yourself from these situations so that they do not become personally devastating. The true challenge is to find the balance within yourself that will enable you to preserve your empathy for your patients and their families while retaining your ability to make solid decisions and continue through your long day with other patients. As a medical student on the wards, you have the opportunity to watch how the more experienced housestaff handle these difficult situations.

Every medical student remembers his or her first experience with death. One told us this story:

It was during my medicine clerkship. My team admitted a patient with a complaint of shortness of breath and chest discomfort. When we first saw him, the patient was very friendly and joking about how he was ready to go home. After he was admitted, we went on to see another patient.

Twenty minutes later we were called by the nurse. The patient was blue and unable to breathe. We ran to his room. The patient looked up at me with fear in his eyes. He said, "I can't breathe. I'm not going to make it. Please keep me alive until morning. Tomorrow's my anniversary." We worked on him for a long time, but we couldn't save him. The patient died right in front of my eyes.

I have never felt so helpless in my life. I ran out of the room to cry. I kept asking myself, "Why couldn't we save him?" My resident followed me out of the room and spoke to me gently. "As a doctor, this will happen many times in your life," he said.

"You have to learn from it and be able to move on. There are other patients on this ward who really need you now." His words helped me compose myself and go on with my work.

Taking a History and Examining Patients

It's one thing to practice patient interaction with volunteers in a classroom setting; it's quite another to encounter your first real live patient in a clinical setting. All your fears and insecurities rise to the surface. The patient will surely know that you are just a lowly medical student, and demand to see an actual doctor. The patient will see how young you look, and demand to see an actual doctor. Or the patient will quickly notice how awkward you feel and how unsure you are of what you're doing, and demand to see an actual doctor. These are the insecurities of every medical student which quickly fade away as patient interaction increases.

As long as you maintain a professional and courteous stance when you approach and interview a patient, you can expect respect and appreciation in return. However, unless you have ever been a hospital or emergency room patient yourself, it is virtually impossible to understand what the person you are treating is going through. Imagine how stressful it is to deal with the unpleasant aspects of hospital care while suffering from a painful, chronic, and/or terminal illness as well. Remember this, and it will keep you from taking a patient's bad mood or surly disposition personally.

Each medical or surgical specialty has its own preferred method of preparing a patient's history and physical exam ("H & P"). Be sure that you understand the way each specialist approaches his or her patient, and why certain parts of the H & P are routinely omitted or included.

There are, however, certain aspects of the history which are universally included. The following list is considered the bare minimum for an inclusive history of a patient for any specialty:

1. Identifying Data (name, age, race, etc.)

2. Chief Complaint (C.C.)

3. History of Present Illness (H.P.I.)

4. Past Medical History (P.M.H.)

5. Psychosocial History

6. Family History

7. Medications and Allergies

8. Review of Systems

The first sentence should include those parts of Identifying Data that are relevant to the situation, including age, gender, race and/or ethnicity, marital status (optional), and profession (optional unless it pertains in some way to the patient's current situation).

The History of Present Illness section should contain a description of the onset of this specific illness or injury, a detailed description of the chief complaint, and any other important information related to the current illness. Any other medical information, including surgical history and a history of injuries and accidents, goes under Past Medical History.

Before you begin the examination itself, ask the patient if he has any questions. You might also ask if there is anything that he can think of that might be important for you to know or that you neglected to ask. Remember to wash your hands before and after the exam, and wear gloves when appropriate to prevent the spread of infection and to protect yourself as well.

The best way to learn to do physical examinations (other than practice), is to watch others on your team examine patients. Take advantage of the opportunity you have as a medical student to observe experienced doctors' styles and methods.

Writing an Admission Note

An admission note explains the purpose of the patient's admission to the hospital. If you have taken the patient history in an organized fashion and jotted down some notes during the process, writing the admission note should be easy, and will soon become routine. In addition to those items that should be included in the patient history, the admission note should include the following:

1-8. Patient history as previously listed

9. Physical examination

10. Emergency room course (if appropriate)

11. Lab values and test results

12. Assessment (includes subjective data, objective data, and case formulation)

13. Differential diagnosis (includes each diagnosis you are entertaining, evidence for and against the diagnosis with discussion)

14. Treatment plan (includes what you plan to do on admission and what you might consider doing in the near future)

The key to writing a good admission note is to be organized. Be sure that you understand the meaning and purpose of each section so that you have emphasized the pertinent pieces of information for that specific patient. The Identifying Data in an admission note should include the reason for admission if it was pre-scheduled or predetermined along with the standard information.

In the Assessment section, outline the case, listing the important aspects of the patient's story and identifying pertinent positive and negative findings which influence your diagnosis. In the next section, you list those diagnoses, in order of the most to least likely, that you are entertaining. The Treatment Plan is also written in list format and includes everything you plan to do while the patient is in the hospital, from tests and procedures to medication and observation.

Reviewing the Hospital Chart

The hospital chart is an important tool for communication among the various disciplines involved in a patient's care. As a medical student, you are usually free to write daily progress notes on patients' charts; however, you may not write medications or any other orders, and you are definitely not allowed to sign any orders.

If you want to familiarize yourself with a patient's condition and history, the best way to do so is to read the chart. If the patient has been in the hospital for a while, the chart may seem like nothing more than a big pile of illegible papers, but if you take the time to sift through them you can gain valuable information.

Start by reading the admission note, then glance through the progress notes page by page. Don't feel compelled to read every word. Instead, follow the intern or prior medical student's notes for important changes in the patient's course, procedures performed, etc.

Then glance at notes from the nurse or the social worker which may contain additional information. Be sure to read any specialty consultations provided during the stay, such as a gynecological consult on a surgical patient or a psychiatric consult on a neurological patient. Finally, look at the orders to identify the medications and doses the patient is currently receiving or has previously received.

The classic inpatient progress note is often referred to as a "SOAP" note, an abbreviation for the following model:

- **S**-Subjective information, or what the patient reports.

- **O**-Objective information, or physical exam findings, vitals, lab values, and other test results, normal and abnormal.

- **A**-Assessment, or a formulating sentence which includes identifying data, diagnosis, subjective reports, and objective findings.

- **P**-Plan, or how you, the physician, will respond to the above information on that day.

Each day you write a SOAP note on each of your patients. Any items listed in your plan section should be transcribed onto a to-do list that you carry around with you so that you are sure to complete the day's work.

Presenting a Patient on Rounds

Every morning, members of the hospital team visit each of their patients and discuss the progress that has been made or complications that have developed. Depending on the specialty through which you are rotating, your colleagues, the housestaff, and the attending on service that month, morning rounds can be either inspirational and educational, or intimidating and uncomfortable. If rounds are unpleasant, just remember that within a few weeks you'll be on another rotation where the experience is bound to get better.

In every rotation, you will be expected to present patients that you have admitted the day or night before, as well as update the team on the progress of those patients under your (supervised) care. It is a good idea to get to the hospital early enough so that you have time to check on each of your patients before rounds. Look at the chart to see if anything happened the night before, check the vital signs through the night, and briefly examine the patient. Also, check on any lab or test results that might have come through since the last time you checked on this patient. These are the details you will be required to present to the team during rounds. Writing this information down on file cards will help you remember these details.

One medical student described his first time presenting a new admission to his team during his rotation through internal medicine:

> *I felt like I knew the patient very well. I had stayed up late the night before reading about the long-term sequelae of diabetes and read and reread my admission note about a hundred times. When it came time to present my knees were knocking and my voice was shaking pretty badly. Thankfully, I knew the answers to the questions the attending asked after my presentation, and he complimented me on my organized approach to the patient's symptoms. Afterward, I told the other medical student on the team how embarrassed I was about my voice shaking. She told me it was completely unnoticeable!*

Being on Call

There is something different, something special, about a hospital at night. There are no visitors milling about, there are no rounds going on. Most of the patients are asleep. Being on call—stationed at the hospital from 5:00 p.m. to 7:00 a.m.—allows you to concentrate, with your intern or resident, on the patient care, admissions, and emergencies that arise during the night. It is usually when you are on call that you are offered the most opportunities to participate in any number of procedures that would be handled by ancillary staff during the day.

Lack of sleep is a definite concern when you're on call. If it's a slow night, you may get several hours of sleep (although not necessarily all in a row). Some nights, you may get no sleep at all. As a medical student, you may not be required to be on call all night. You may get to go home at midnight. Even so, you may feel it necessary to do some reading on the case that you admitted that night in order to be prepared for early morning rounds, which means you will still suffer from lack of sleep. Your body will build tolerance to this sleep deficit; it is an unpleasant fact of a prospective doctor's life, but it is survivable.

One medical student whose chosen field was dermatology was not looking forward to her surgical rotation where she knew she'd be on call. She told us:

> *I was determined to hate surgery. I was exhausted by the thought of what I was expected to do. We were allowed to go home at midnight, but were expected to be back in the hospital for 5:00 a.m. rounds. Since I lived forty-five minutes from the hospital, I decided it wasn't worth going home. Staying overnight, I found I was given the opportunity to do many things I would not otherwise have done, including scrubbing in for an emergency GI bleed and getting a front row seat while I held the retractor from 3:00 a.m. to 5:00 a.m. It turned out to be a great learning experience. I proved to myself that I could handle a surgeon's schedule (for two months, anyway), and I got honors in the clerkship to boot!*

A New Way of Learning: Study Skills for the Wards, Exams, and Grades

Believe it or not, the third year actually competes with the first two basic science years of medical school for the Information Overload award. Not only will the environment seem totally foreign to you, but so will the material and the way in which it is presented. For the most part, classroom studies are behind you. Most of your learning will be through observation.

You will be tempted to take notes while you are on the wards. Every conversation between housestaff on rounds or during conferences or lectures will offer new information that in some way integrates facts you have learned in the first two years with some clinical situation. Don't pressure yourself to get every tidbit of knowledge onto paper. Just let yourself listen. Almost everything you hear is available to you in textbooks and journal articles. You can always look up answers to questions you find particularly interesting.

There may be times when you do want to jot down a key piece of information. Once again, file cards that fit in your pocket are the perfect solution. Later, these cards can act as study guides for testing yourself on various topics when you have the time. Be selective when incorporating minutiae into your study materials; pay particular attention to those topics or facts that are repeated by your teachers, attending, or residents.

The exams given during the third and fourth years rarely have the significance or influence on your grade that the exams of the first two years have. You will also find that you don't need to spend as much time memorizing as in the past. Third-year exams will have fewer multiple choice questions and more essays and oral interview-style questions. It's a good idea to talk to fourth-year students to find out what you can expect on these exams.

Your grades during the third year of medical school may prove to be the most important grades for your transcript. You should not be devastated if you don't get an honors grade in every rotation, but you must get an average or passing grade. If you know that you want to pursue a certain field, it is worth your while to work hard and do your best during that rotation. You want to get more than a good grade—you also want to get a glowing evaluation to incorporate into your residency application. If you are entertaining a number of specialty possibilities, it's even more important that you do your best, because you don't know whose recommendation you might need down the road.

The key to a solid grade and good recommendation in all rotations, from psychiatry to surgery, is your genuine interest in learning whatever anyone has to teach you. Your willingness to work with others as a team player, to tolerate difficult, stressful situations with grace, and to respect your patients and the specialty under which they are being treated, will clearly shine through. When you receive a clerkship grade and written evaluation, take the opportunity to feel proud of yourself for those good qualities which are addressed, and to learn from any constructive criticism that is included.

Finding a Mentor

One of the most valuable aspects of being on rotation is the opportunity to meet and make connections with respected, experienced professionals. It is also your opportunity to find one or more mentors. A mentor is defined as a "wise and trusted counselor." This is someone to whom you can talk about your progress as a medical student, someone who can help you make difficult decisions, someone who can generally encourage you and support your efforts.

A mentor need not be trained in the specialty you are considering, although she can usually refer you to people in your specialty you may be interested in meeting. One first-year resident told us that her mentor was the faculty advisor for the medical student journal she was editing with other classmates.

> *I remember talking to Dr. J about everything I was experiencing in medical school, from the difficult exam I had taken that day to the article I was editing for the journal, to where I was going on vacation. Even though I applied for residencies in psychiatry, and Dr. J was a pathologist, I asked him to write a letter of recommendation for me. He seemed delighted to do this, and I was told later by many who had read this letter that it was extremely supportive and unusual, coming from someone with whom I had worked on an extracurricular project. Dr. J's mentorship and friendship during medical school was a key component of my success during that time.*

CHAPTER 6

The Third Year

WHAT YOU CAN EXPECT

Your days of sitting in big lecture halls are over. Although lectures are still given during your rotations, the focus is now on patient care. And as you will learn, the major responsibility for your education is in your hands. There is much less structure in the third year than there was in the first two years. It is important, therefore, to be both assertive and aggressive, but not obnoxious. The more desire and interest in learning you show, the more positive the feedback you will get. Don't be afraid to ask questions. The residents and attendings usually respond better to students who show initiative.

Most students find their clerkship years much more enjoyable than the basic sciences. Each school has its own policy with regard to choosing third year clerkships. You may be able to set up your own schedule. Hospitals and/or rotations may be assigned to you, or selected through a lottery system. If your school is affiliated with several different types of hospitals (community, private, public), take advantage of this opportunity and try to experience each of them. If there is only one hospital available to you, take advantage of everything it has to offer.

Charity Hospital is in need of as many helping hands as possible, which affords even inexperienced medical students the chance for a lot of hands-on experience with patient care, tests, and procedures.

**Medical student, Louisiana State University
School of Medicine in New Orleans**

The more exposure you get to various rotations in the third year, the better position you'll be in to make a career decision. Before deciding where to do your clerkships, talk to upperclassmen and get their advice. Having already been through the system, their experiences can provide you with valuable insights and information.

By the time you've finished your third year, you will need to decide what kind of doctor you want to be. So keep an open mind while doing your rotations. Not only will your clerkships be more enjoyable, you'll get much more out of the experience. Even if you've had your heart set on being a proctologist since nursery school, it's important to get as much as you can out of each rotation. This may be your last opportunity to get hands-on experience in the areas you don't choose to pursue—so take advantage of the time you have.

As stated in the last chapter, during your third year of medical school you will have rotations in the following required clerkships:

- Internal Medicine
- General Surgery
- Obstetrics and Gynecology
- Pediatrics
- Psychiatry

Some schools also require additional rotations such as Neurology, Geriatrics, or Family Practice. There are as many variations on third and fourth year programs as there are medical schools. Each school has developed its own curriculum for juniors and seniors; here are just a few examples of the kinds of programs you may find:

- During their junior year at Texas A&M University College of Medicine, in addition to spending most of their time completing clerkships in the major disciplines and family medicine, students must also take courses that introduce diagnostic instruments. Although much of the fourth year is free for electives, seniors work for six weeks each in neurology and in an alcohol and drug dependence program. Students are also required to attend lectures in medical jurisprudence, biostatistics, epidemiology, public health, and medical humanities.

- An unusual feature of Boston University's School of Medicine is the required clerkship in Home Medical Service, in which students are responsible for primary care of geriatric patients.

- Students at the University of Kansas School of Medicine must work for one month with a practicing community physician, a requirement that is normally fulfilled in a small-town setting.

- At Tulane University School of Medicine, a four-week community medicine clerkship is mandatory; students may choose to complete this requirement in locations as mundane as rural Oklahoma or as exotic as Belize.

- At the Mayo Medical School, the third year is divided into two segments: clerkships and the research semester. In the clerkship portion, students go though intensive rotations in internal medicine, obstetrics and gynecology, surgery, neurology, and pediatrics. During the research semester, they investigate topics of particular interest, write formal research papers, and present their findings.

CLINICAL ROTATIONS

Internal Medicine

Internal medicine is the study of the organ systems with emphasis on disease and treatment. An internist is a physician who specializes in the diagnosis and nonsurgical treatment of diseases in adults. When people think of a physician, they often envision an internist, a doctor who cares for a wide variety of medical problems. On this rotation, you will be involved with caring for people with common (and not so common) medical ailments.

The rotation itself lasts from two to three months. The time is divided between inpatient and outpatient (ambulatory) care. Inpatient care involves working as part of the team of intern, resident, and attending physician tending to the care of patients admitted to the hospital. Outpatient care involves seeing patients in a clinic setting. This is similar to people visiting their doctors in the office. In each setting, you will be exposed to continuity of care, enabling you to follow patients through all stages of illness—sickness, recovery, and health.

When you're on this rotation, get ready to do battle! You will be sent directly to the front line. Your day will be full of duties, tasks, and new adventures. Most of your morning will be spent on rounds; don't take them for granted. Although you will be quizzed on your presentation and general knowledge, this is your opportunity to pick the brains of the housestaff and attending. Make sure you know your patients and understand their medical problems. Learn the different stages of the disease process, including etiology (the cause), pathogenesis (the development), manifestations (physical evidence), and treatment.

After rounds are completed, the afternoons are usually filled with conferences, lectures, and floor work. Conferences involve discussions covering relevant medical topics, given by the housestaff or attendings. Lectures are given specifically to medical students, and deal with various topics deemed important for the knowledge of internal medicine. Floor work includes checking lab results, drawing blood, ordering tests and procedures, writing progress notes, and working up new admissions. Unless you're on call, the day usually ends with sign-out, when you review with the resident the day's events for patients under your care.

Out-patient care, on the other hand, is not as structured. The time in the clinic is spent seeing patients with a wide variety of medical problems. For each patient you see (under the supervision of the housestaff), you should first review the chart, which gives you a history of the problem and other related information. Once this is done, you see your patient, doing a focused history and physical. Afterwards, you present the patient and discuss the treatment plan and follow-up with the attending. You will find that as soon as you're finished with one patient, you have another waiting for you.

In most medical schools, your grade consists of two parts: a clinical grade and an exam grade. The clinical grade is based on your performance on the wards. The exam grade is based on your score on a written section and a practical section. The practical section assesses the skills required in the practice of internal medicine:

- history-taking
- physical exam

- differential diagnosis
- reading chest X rays
- interpreting EKGs
- reading urine samples
- reviewing Gram stains and blood smears
- evaluating heart sounds

While on the wards, it is important to get as much exposure to these skills as you can. The more practice you get, the better prepared you will be for the practical. You can always ask the housestaff and attending for help; they are there to teach, as well as to take care of patients.

Internal medicine is the backbone of all medical practice. Skills you learn during this rotation are applicable no matter what field you go into. Get the most out of this rotation by seeing as many patients as you can, and by doing as many procedures as you are able.

Surgery

Surgery is concerned with diseases or conditions requiring operative or manual procedures. Some students consider the rotation in surgery to be the most difficult of the third year. The days are long; you come in early and stay late; while at the hospital, you're constantly on the move. Down-time is rare.

The rotation lasts from two to three months (depending on your school). This clerkship is divided between general surgery and the subspecialties, which consist of:

- Urology
- Orthopedics
- Neurosurgery
- Ophthalmology
- Cardiothoracic
- Plastics
- Pediatrics

Depending on your school, you may or may not have the opportunity to experience all of them. Again, you will be involved in both inpatient and outpatient care. On the inpatient service, you'll be taking care of patients on the wards, in the operating rooms, and in the ICU (intensive care unit). The outpatient service consists of working in the clinic and with elective surgery cases. In addition, you'll be attending conferences and lectures.

As you did in your internal medicine clerkship, you will be working in a team setting. Unlike internal medicine, however, your day is not structured. Rounds are short, involving a quick check of the patients before the OR day begins. Your day basically revolves around the OR; the rest of your time will be divided between floor work and working up your patients. The floor work includes checking lab results, drawing blood, placing IVs, changing bandages, removing sutures, and other minor procedures. Working up your patients involves taking complete histories and physicals and writing daily progress notes.

Time in the clinic will be similar to that spent in internal medicine. You will see many patients with acute problems, and you will be performing follow-up post surgery. Additionally, you may be performing minor surgical procedures under housestaff supervision. As in medicine, it's important to review the chart before getting started. After examining the patient, you will present the case to the attending and discuss how the case will be managed.

Before your first visit to the operating room, you are likely to be apprehensive. This is entirely normal. It can be an intimidating experience, because, even in minor surgery, a life is hanging in the balance. The attending, a resident, yourself, and a few scrub nurses will be crowded around the table. There are rules of etiquette that must be followed. You are not there to do surgery. You are there primarily to observe and assist in the operation. This usually means holding retractors and cutting sutures. Some doctors may actually let you make a small incision or sew an incision closed. Some will teach as the procedure goes on; others will expect you to learn purely by observation. One medical student relayed his experience during his surgery rotation:

> *I think of Dr. Jekyll and Mr. Hyde every time I think of this attending physician. On the ward, he was always approachable and eager to help students. He went out of his way, at times,*

to make sure we understood important concepts in surgery. Then one day, I was to assist on a case with this surgeon. To my disbelief, he turned into a fearsome and diabolical monster. He screamed over the smallest things. He yelled at everyone in the OR. He had no interest in teaching the medical students. I was there to retract, nothing else.

After the operation was over, "Dr. Jekyll" came over and asked me if I had any questions about the procedure. I didn't know what to say. From that day on, I made sure I never ran into "Mr. Hyde" in the OR again. "Dr. Jekyll," however, was the best teacher I ever had.

The most important thing to remember about surgery is that a sterile operating field is of prime importance. Scrubbing in is a requirement before any OR procedure. This includes washing your hands, wearing your gown, and not being contaminated during surgery. You will be carefully initiated into this process before your first surgery.

Once you are scrubbed, gowned, and gloved, you are ready to enter the "zone of no return." Because you may be standing for a long period of time, it is advisable to wear comfortable shoes and to eat beforehand. Once the operation begins, you won't be allowed to take a break.

Not all doctors are like the one described above. Many will use the opportunity to pump you on your knowledge of the operating procedure at hand. You can prepare by studying the anatomy, pathology, indications for surgery, treatments, and possible complications of the cases in which you participate. Don't forget that the purpose of this clerkship is to acquire the basic knowledge of surgical principles; you do not have to learn the specific details of surgical procedures.

Because of the demanding schedule you will face, it is important to stay on top of your reading material. Not only do you need to know general surgery, but all the subspecialties as well. Your grade in surgery, as in medicine, consists of two parts: clinical and exam. The clinical grade is based on your performance on the wards. Your exam grade is based on your performance on a written test of both your general knowledge and your reasoning capacity in surgery. Some schools also require a research paper and a presentation on a relevant surgical topic.

Surgery is an intensive and exhausting rotation involving long hours and mastery of a difficult subject. Nonetheless, it is a very rewarding experience. Whether you decide to become a surgeon or not, procedures you learn here will have application in any field you enter (for instance, every doctor needs to know how to suture). As you follow patients from admission to OR to discharge, you will gain a basic understanding of the progression of disease and its treatment. Most students have strong feelings about surgery: they love it or hate it. Either way, it's bound to be one of the most memorable experiences of your medical school career.

Obstetrics/Gynecology

Obstetrics is concerned with the care of women during pregnancy. Gynecology is the medical specialty concerned with the diseases of the genital tract and the reproductive physiology of the female. As a student, this is your opportunity to deliver a baby and to learn about issues dealing with women's health.

This clerkship lasts from six to eight weeks. The time is divided evenly between obstetrics and gynecology. During obstetrics, you will spend time on labor and delivery, on the wards, and in the prenatal care clinic. During gynecology, you will spend time on the wards, in the OR, and in the clinic.

You will find this course to be different from your other rotations. OB/GYN is a combination of medicine and surgery. It combines the continuity of care that is provided by medicine with the operating room experience of surgery. Surgery isn't the only rotation that demands long hours. OB/GYN rounds begin very early in the morning, and the day can last from twelve to fourteen hours. But unlike surgery, there is down-time while you wait for deliveries.

Once people know you're a medical student, the most common question they ask is, "Have you ever delivered a baby?" After you complete this rotation, you can certainly answer, "Yes." For many students, delivering a baby is the highlight of their medical school years.

I couldn't believe what I had just witnessed. What a feeling—to see a baby come out—it's simply amazing. They come out head first, and just plop right into your hands. They're so...alive. There are no words to describe how beautiful, how awesome that experience can be.

Medical student, New York Medical College

During obstetrics, you'll be spending time on labor and delivery, on the wards, and in the prenatal/postpartum clinic. Your days usually begin by checking the delivery board, a blackboard on which patient information is displayed which will tell you if any patients are about to give birth. The rest of the day is scheduled around deliveries. When you're not aiding in deliveries, you will be involved with rounds, clinic, scut work, conferences, lectures, and occasional trips to the OR.

Rounds, again, are a team effort. You and the team will be checking patients in labor and delivery and on the wards. Rounds are usually short and to the point. As in your other rotations, you should be prepared to present your patients. After rounds, you will be doing floor work and scut. This includes working up patients, placing IVs, drawing blood, and delivering babies.

Once in a while, you will have the opportunity to scrub in on a cesarean section. Like any other OR procedure, the rules of etiquette and sterility apply. During the operation, you will be assisting the surgeon by holding the clamps while the surgeon removes the infant. Toward the end of your rotation, you may be allowed to assist the surgeon in closing the c-section incision.

The rest of your time in obstetrics will be in the clinic. Here, you will be able to follow both prenatal and postnatal courses. Patients come in for routine checkups or to address complications affecting their pregnancy. In addition, you will see patients for follow-up after they have given birth.

During gynecology, you have the opportunity to spend time on the floor, in the OR, and in the clinic. Your day again begins with rounds. These rounds are no different from OB, except that these women aren't pregnant. The rest of your day is spent either in OR, in the clinic, in lectures, or in conferences.

You will spend a lot of time in the clinic in gynecology. For some women, the gynecologist is their primary care physician. Keep in mind that if you are male, you are required to have a female chaperone with you when examining your patient. There are no exceptions to this rule. This is for your protection and for the patient's comfort.

In clinic, be prepared to see a wide range of medical problems, including sexually transmitted diseases, AIDS, cancer, birth control needs, and simple infections. Depending on your program and the hospital at which you are doing your rotations, you may have the opportunity to observe an abortion. Medical schools do not require any student to participate in this procedure. You will, however, assist in many dilations and curettages (D and C's), a common operation to remove abnormal tissue lining the uterus.

As in other rotations, it is important to integrate things you learn in the hospital with your studying at home. Divide your time equally between obstetrics and gynecology. As in surgery, don't get bogged down in details. You will receive a clinical grade and an exam grade once again. In some schools, an oral exam may also be given.

Obstetrics and gynecology is an attractive field to many students because it combines aspects of primary care with surgical procedures. In addition, this is the only specialty in which you have to take care of two patients at the same time: mother and child. Most importantly, this is the only rotation where you get to bring a new life into the world, one of the greatest rewards of being a doctor.

Pediatrics

For many students, even those who have no intention of pursuing this specialty, pediatrics is their favorite rotation. The environment in the pediatrics ward is often more relaxed and cheerful than the other hospital wards. However, pediatrics can be depressing as well. It is not easy to see a child who is facing an invasive surgical procedure or who has a terminal illness. On the other hand, it is thrilling to know that you and your team have enabled a sick child to recover and grow into adulthood.

As a third-year medical student, you will be in a position to observe everything that goes on in pediatrics without the pressure to perform. You will be assigned patients and will probably take call and participate in admissions, but you have fewer responsibilities in pediatrics than in other rotations. For obvious reasons, pediatricians are protective of the well-being of their patients, and prefer that they be cared for by more experienced hands (at least for infants, toddlers, and young children). You will be called upon to do a lot of hand-holding, however. At most schools, the pediatrics rotation lasts two months.

If you have younger siblings, or have done a lot of babysitting, you'll have no trouble feeling comfortable in pediatrics. If you have limited experience with young people, you might want to use this opportunity to observe how the residents and attendings communicate with children of varying ages. You can't deal with a five-year-old in the same manner as you would an eleven-year-old. If you choose to pursue a career in this field, this aspect of your training will prove invaluable.

One of the unique aspects of pediatrics is that you will have greater interaction with the patient's family. Often, parents present a more difficult challenge than the patients do. It is not unusual for a mother to rush into the emergency room, screaming hysterically that her daughter has been seriously injured. Upon examination, you often find that the little girl, who is not even crying, has only scraped her knee and needs nothing more than a good cleaning and a Band-Aid.

Another aspect unique to pediatrics is that the illnesses you see are often specific to that field. Although there are certainly child and adult versions of the same diagnoses, such as diabetes mellitus or tuberculosis, there are many diseases unique to children. For this reason, pediatrics has its own series of sub-specialties, each of which you can explore in detail. Then, in your fourth year, you might choose to pursue an elective in one of these fields for a more in-depth experience.

It's easy to understand how pediatrics can be a rewarding experience. As one medical student shared with us:

> *I was in clinic and my first patient for the day came into the room with his mother. The boy was about six years old and very quiet. He stared at me the whole time and watched every move I made. Before I examined him, he leaned over to his mother and whispered something. The mother then told the child to tell me what he said. He was too shy, and turned red. His mother looked at me and said, "He wants to become a doctor, just like you." Suddenly, I was six years old again, looking up at my pediatrician and thinking those very words. I could only hope that this little boy would be able to realize his dreams, as I was realizing mine.*

Psychiatry

Like the pediatrics rotation, the psychiatry rotation is usually two months, significantly shorter than the internal medicine rotation. One of the younger fields of medicine, psychiatry is the science of treating mental disease. In the psychiatry rotation, as in pediatrics, your role is to learn by observation. You will have many opportunities to watch psychiatric residents interview patients on the wards, in the out-patient clinic, and in the emergency room. Eventually, you will get to practice the psychiatric interview and mental status examination yourself.

Psychiatry also offers many subspecialties, including such emerging fields as consult liaison and child/adolescent psychiatry. Consult liaison psychiatry is a subspecialty that deals with a psychiatrist's involvement with a psychiatric patient who is being treated for a medical illness. Child/adolescent psychiatry incorporates working with families and teachers as well as children. The newest areas of interest in this subspecialty involve psychopharmacology geared specifically for children.

You will probably have a number of lectures during your rotation in psychiatry, and you may be surprised by the number of different orientations to which you will be introduced. Whereas one lecturer may speak to you about the value of strict psychoanalysis and the theories of Sigmund Freud, another may advocate the use of psycho-pharmacological management with little or no support from psycho-therapy. A third lecturer may combine the two viewpoints.

A medical student who spent his rotation in the psychiatric emergency room of a large hospital in New York City told us:

> *What I liked most about psychiatry was that I could finally sit down with a patient for an extended period of time and really get the story in detail while I observed everything about her, including how she delivered the story, and how she appeared. Strangely enough, I felt more like a doctor in this rotation than in the others, where the patient seemed to take a back seat to other responsibilities in the hospital.*

You probably learn more in your third year of medical school than in the first two years combined. The experiences you have working in the hospital give you the background and preparation you need for your success as a physician. In addition, you develop your own preferences regarding each clerkship, which will prove invaluable in deciding on a medical specialty.

CHAPTER 7

The Fourth Year

WHAT YOU CAN EXPECT

Most students agree that this is the best year of medical school. The hardest parts are behind you. You've memorized, forgotten, and relearned thousands of new terms, ideas, concepts, and procedures. You've survived the most difficult courses and passed the worst exams. You've familiarized yourself with the hospital, its layout, staff, and rules of etiquette, and have overcome many of the feelings of uncertainty and insecurity that come with being a "stranger in a strange land."

The fourth year is a time of choice and change. Although you will still have some required rotations to complete, you will also have a great deal of freedom in choosing electives and the direction your medical life will take.

Required courses in the fourth year generally include:

- Subinternship (medicine/pediatrics/surgery)
- Geriatrics
- Ambulatory Care/Generalist
- Neurology

In some schools, you are required to take none of these courses; some or all may be required at others. Some of these courses may have been completed in your third year. Certain schools may require additional coursework in such areas as family practice, surgical subspecialties, clinical pharmacology, community health, emergency medicine, radiology and research. All schools leave you plenty of time in the fourth year to take electives, which means that you choose the areas of specialty you would like to study.

By the time the fourth year begins, you should have some idea of your choice of specialty. During the first month of the year, you will make a tentative career choice and begin requesting applications to residency programs. Remember, though, that no choice is irrevocable until you sign the residency contract. The choice you make will be your guide in setting up your fourth-year schedule and in choosing electives.

As the fall approaches, the application process goes into full swing (see the next chapter for full details). By now, you should have narrowed down your specialty choices. The application process can actually be an enjoyable and interesting experience. When you interview at various programs, you will have the opportunity to visit new places and meet new people, whether you are going across town or to another part of the country.

The schedule for your fourth year has several components, including:

- required rotations
- electives
- interview appointments
- study time for the National Boards
- vacation

Some students prefer to take required courses first, to get them out of the way. This allows you more free time at the end of the year. However, if you are interested in a particular specialty, it's probably a good idea to take that rotation early in the year. Courses taken early show up on your transcript and dean's letter, which get sent to residency programs to which you are applying. You may also want to get letters of recommendation from doctors in these specialties to include with your applications. Be aware that availability in some electives may be limited, or the elective may only be offered during certain time periods, so it's important to plan ahead.

You must also set aside time for interviewing, studying for the National Boards, and vacationing. Depending on the residency for which you apply, interviewing will take place in late fall or early winter. You should schedule time off accordingly. The National Boards are given twice a year—late summer and early spring, so you must adjust your schedule to allow time for studying. Finally, and perhaps most importantly, schedule vacation time for yourself (and your family, if applicable). Opportunities for vacationing during residency training are few and far between. You need, and deserve, time to recharge your batteries before you begin the next phase of your medical career.

REQUIRED COURSES

Subinternship

Subinternships are additional rotations in specialties you have previously covered, including medicine, pediatrics, and surgery. Required courses usually last from two to four weeks, and are geared to teaching you to think and act like an intern. As a subintern, you are given more responsibility and less spoon-feeding than you had as a third-year student. Although your notes and orders have to be co-signed, you work up patients as any first-year physician would.

Third year concentrates on the illnesses and problems of the patient, with emphasis on learning to do a history and physical and develop a differential diagnosis. Fourth year takes this a step farther and teaches patient management. You'll learn treatment modalities, including drug dosages and ordering appropriate tests and procedures. You will spend your fourth year fine-tuning your clinical skills. You are expected to apply the knowledge base that you built during your third year and improve on it.

Many of the fourth-year courses include lectures and conferences. Some may require an exam, a paper, or a presentation. For the most part, however, grades are based solely on clinical performance.

During your subinternship, you will be functioning much like an intern. You will be responsible for caring for your own patients, with a resident supervisor. You can expect a lot of work and long hours. The original definition of an intern was "someone who resides in a hospital." This is not far from the truth. It may seem as if you never get to go home. Your day usually begins with pre-round assessment of patients under your care. During rounds, you will be quizzed and questioned extensively by the resident and attending. After rounds, the day is spent in floor work and in working up new admissions. You will get a beeper—which will become your greatest enemy. As one fourth-year student told us:

I was so excited the day I got my own beeper. It made me feel like a real doctor for the first time. I actually paged myself a few times, enthralled with the sound of the beeper. This feeling did not last long. By the end of my first day as a subintern, I was paged so many times I just wanted to throw the thing away.

One early morning, as I lay in bed, I heard that horrible paging sound and I jumped up to get to the phone, when I suddenly realized that the sound was coming from my alarm clock. It had the same tone and ringing sequence as my pager! Without thinking twice, I slammed the alarm clock into a thousand pieces. I wished I could do the same with my beeper.

The subinternship is truly your transition between medical school and internship. It gives you a taste of what is to come, both in terms of duties and in increased responsibility.

Geriatrics

Geriatrics is a specialty of medicine concerned with the medical care of the elderly. As the elderly population continues to grow in this country, geriatrics has come to the forefront of medicine. You will be applying what you learned in internal medicine to the special needs and problems of the elderly.

The care of the elderly does not end in the hospital. Treatment extends to home care and nursing homes, as many patients are no longer self-sufficient and require additional assistance. They receive aid in the form of home attendants or nurses. Since many of these patients are not ambulatory, doctors make house calls and nursing home visits.

This is a unique experience. As a student, you have the opportunity to visit patients in their home environments, which allows you to asses them, both medically and socially, from a broader perspective. By gaining a fuller understanding of these patients, it is it possible to make a more informed decision about their medical care.

As the elderly population continues to grow, geriatrics is becoming an increasingly important field. By the year 2020, more than 20 percent of the United States' population will be over sixty-five years of age. Therefore, no matter what field of medicine you decide to enter (other than pediatrics), you will probably have geriatric patients under your care.

Ambulatory Care/Generalist

Ambulatory care/generalist is a rotation concerned with outpatient medicine. This is a change of pace from your other clerkships, which dealt primarily with inpatient care. Here, your primary responsibility is with patients in a clinic or office setting. This is an important rotation, as the majority of patients see doctors in these settings.

Ambulatory care gives you the opportunity to see a variety of medical problems. In many cases, the clinic doctor is the patient's primary care physician, which means this is where they come whether their medical problems are large or small. This rotation gives you an excellent overview of the everyday medical concerns of the community at large.

Ambulatory care runs on a more "normal" schedule than other rotations. The day usually begins about 8:30 a.m. or 9:00 a.m. and finishes around 5:00 p.m., or whenever you've seen your last patient. In between, there is little down time, as clinics are often overcrowded and booked for weeks in advance—which means that you will be seeing one patient right after another.

A generalist rotation gives you a different kind of outpatient experience. Instead of working in a clinic, you're primarily exposed to patient care in a private physician's office. The day is spent following the doctor around as she tends to patients in her office. Your hours and your responsibilities will vary depending on the physician.

As a whole, these rotations are more representative of medicine in the real world. It is to your advantage, therefore, to make the most out of them. Right now, there is a shortage of general practice physicians in this country, and a great emphasis on family care and generalist training in medical schools.

Neurology

Neurology is the study of the disorders that affect the nervous system. This course is an extension of the neuroscience course covered during the basic science years, but now clinical application is emphasized. Neurologists use many tests and procedures in the treatment of their patients, and you will be expected to become familiar with them all, including the MRI and the CT scan; the PET (positron emission tomography) scan, an enhanced CAT scan which images brain blood flow and function; electromyography (EMG), which yields information about muscles and nerves; and the electroencephalogram (EEG), which reports brain wave activity.

The goal of this rotation is to familiarize you with diseases of the nervous system and their management. Here, you will learn to administer neurological and mental status exams, for which you will use the tuning fork, reflex hammer, and pen light you purchased during your second year.

The majority of time in this rotation is spent in inpatient wards, doing rounds and discussing patients. You will see patients with problems ranging from head trauma to neurological diseases like myasthenia gravis and multiple sclerosis. When you are not on the wards, you will be in the emergency room and in the ambulatory setting.

Your outpatient experience will expose you to common neurological problems such as headaches, seizures, and episodes of dizziness and fainting. These problems can be just as serious as major neurological diseases. Learning how to diagnose and treat these common conditions will be invaluable no matter what field you enter.

ELECTIVES

During the fourth year, you will have the freedom to choose rotations in a variety of specialties outside the medical school requirements. When setting up an elective schedule, try to balance more rigorous rotations, such as emergency medicine, with easier alternatives, such as ophthalmology or dermatology. An optimal fourth year combines a little of both.

Depending on your school, you may have the opportunity to do electives anywhere in the world. Use this opportunity to broaden your horizons. You could spend a month working with a world-famous physician, or practice medicine in the most remote regions of the Amazon River. Remember that the opportunity to travel and explore new ideas and options may not be available to you again for quite some time.

It is important to keep your ultimate goal in mind when making your choices. There are five basic reasons for choosing particular electives:

1. Interest in a specialty

2. Making a career choice

3. Auditioning at a program

4. Preparing for residency

5. Strengthening your transcript

1. Interest in a specialty

Many students use fourth year as a tool to expand their knowledge by learning about subjects not otherwise covered in the curriculum. Once you begin your residency, you will no longer have the opportunity to take electives outside of your chosen specialty. This may be your last chance to get a taste of a particular type of medicine that interests you, even though you have no desire to pursue it professionally. For instance, if you've decided on a career in pediatrics, you may want to take a rotation in geriatrics simply because it may be your last opportunity to work with elderly patients.

2. Making a career choice

If you are having trouble deciding on a postgraduate career, exposing yourself to several different electives may be the answer. This gives you an opportunity to experience a specialty you may not know that much about and decide whether or not you would be happy pursuing a career in that direction. You gain an appreciation of how the specialty works, the kinds of patients you'll see, and the lifestyle this specialty affords. Although a month is a short period of time, it can still serve as the foundation for your career choice. Many students have reconsidered career choices after getting a taste of the inner workings of a specialty.

3. Auditioning at a program

You may choose to do an elective program where you would like to do your residency training. Some students use their elective time to showcase their talent. There are advantages and disadvantages to this strategy. It is an opportunity to introduce yourself and show program directors that you are intelligent, hardworking, and a team player. This may be an important advantage in a highly competitive program.

Another benefit of choosing an elective at a program of your choice is to get a realistic impression of what the residency is like. You work intimately with residents and attendings who will be your future colleagues. In addition, you learn about the inner workings of the hospital and the surrounding area.

The disadvantage is that, particularly in the more popular programs, other students will be auditioning as well. Competition may be fierce. This makes it difficult for you to shine, and more likely that small mistakes will be noticed. A poor showing during this rotation may eliminate you from consideration.

4. Preparing for residency

Fourth year gives you an opportunity to hone your clinical skills and enhance your knowledge base in your chosen field. You may be anxious to get a head start and prepare for your upcoming residency. For example, students entering medicine may want to sharpen their skills in reading EKGs and X rays. Those entering surgery may want to do a month in the intensive care unit or on the trauma team. During these rotations, you will gain skills and techniques important for your field of study.

5. Strengthening your transcript

Applications for residency, like applications for medical school, require that you submit several letters of recommendation. There is no better way to get to know respected physicians in your field of choice than to do a rotation with them. Once you get to know the doctor personally, you can ask for his help in getting accepted to the residency program.

Research

Some schools require that you spend time doing research; others offer research as an elective for those who are interested. Research is an excellent way to gain firsthand knowledge of the scientific method, which allows you to take a theory and, from it, develop a hypothesis, which is then proven or disproven through experimentation. This method of scientific thought is a skill required of all physicians. It is especially critical to be able to gather and interpret data. Since medicine is an ever-changing field, new discoveries are being made every day. As a physician, you will constantly be called upon to study and evaluate such material and judge its relevance to treating your patients. A background in research and an appreciation of the scientific method allows you to do this in an informed and intelligent manner.

Research in your chosen specialty can strengthen your transcript by showing residency programs your true interest and initiative in that field. In addition, any published articles or papers with your name on them will greatly enhance your resume.

CHAPTER 8

Planning for Residency

WHAT YOU CAN EXPECT

Just when you start feeling comfortable with medical school and all its idiosyncrasies, it's time to move on. One minute you're scrubbing in on a case, and the next minute, you're sending out residency applications. As you now begin to realize, your medical school training is just the beginning. The true process of becoming a doctor takes place during your internship and residency.

A resident is basically an apprentice doctor. Residents are trained at teaching hospitals throughout the United States. Training lasts from three to seven years, depending on your specialty. During this time you will earn approximately $25,000 to $35,000 a year and work anywhere from sixty to one hundred and twenty hours a week—often with no days off.

A first-year resident is known as an intern. This experience is similar to entering high school from junior high—you step out of a world where you are top gun and step into a world where you are low man (or woman) on the totem pole. Your internship is similar to your third year of medical school in that you will be doing rotations. For instance, as an intern in general surgery, you may spend half your year training in general surgery, and the other six months in rotations in plastic surgery, thoracic surgery, orthopedic surgery, transplant surgery, etc.

You will spend a lot of time on call, perhaps as often as every third or fourth night. As the residency program progresses, the amount of time you spend on call decreases. Some residencies, such as radiology and dermatology, rarely require you to be on call, or allow you to have home call, so you can be beeped from your home as opposed to having to stay at the hospital overnight.

The amount of training you have ahead of you depends on your choice of specialty. For instance, if you want to become a dermatologist, you will have to train for one year as an intern and three years as a resident. If you want to become an oncologist (a doctor who specializes in treating cancer), you will train for one year as an intern and two years as a resident in internal medicine, followed by a three-year fellowship in oncology. (See Appendix I for a list of specialties and training required for each.)

How do you know what residencies are available to you? Every school's graduate education office has a copy of the *Graduate Medical Education Dictionary*, issued annually by the American Medical Association (also known as "The Green Book"), which lists all the residency programs accredited by the Accreditation Council for Graduate Medical Education. The AMA has also developed a computer program called *The Fellowship and Residency Electronic Interactive Database Access* (FREIDA) that contains complete information on all residency programs.

You can also use the *NRMP Directory*, published yearly by the National Resident Matching Program. If you sign up for the Match, you will receive this book in the mail, but you can also find copies in the school's library or education office. Information is also available by writing to associations pertaining to the specialty in which you are interested. For example, if you're looking for residency programs in anesthesiology, you can get information from the American Board of Anesthesiology or the American Society of Anesthesiologists (see Appendix I for further details).

One of the best ways to find out about residencies is to ask upperclassmen who have already gone through the search process. You can also ask doctors who are currently practicing in a specialty what residency programs they recommend.

Two books you may find helpful during your application process are *Getting Into a Residency–A Guide for Medical Students* and *Resumes and Personal Statements for Health Professionals* (see Appendix II for details).

Applying for residency is a complicated, tedious process which can be made easier by organization and forethought. The process actually begins in the third year of medical school, when you should begin thinking about career choices and letters of recommendation. As you complete each third-year clerkship, ask physicians with whom you've worked, or who know you well, to write you a letter of recommendation. It's best to ask while you are still fresh in their minds; they may not remember you as clearly by the time the next mob of students rolls in.

The application process is made up of several steps, including:

- getting letters of recommendation
- requesting and completing residency applications
- registering for the Match
- writing a curriculum vitae (resume) and a personal statement
- requesting a Dean's Letter/Chairman's Letter
- arranging and going on interviews
- choosing programs
- entering a rank order list

Most of the application process takes place during your fourth year, which means you need to take this into consideration when setting up your schedule. You'll need time to complete applications and write your curriculum vitae and personal statement. You'll also need days off to attend interviews.

You are responsible for sending completed applications, CVs, and personal statements to each program to which you are applying. Student Affairs will send transcripts, Dean's Letters, National Board scores, and any letters of recommendation. Make sure that Student Affairs has the correct address of all programs you are considering. Once programs receive all your information, they will consider your candidacy. Qualified candidates will then be invited for an interview.

As the interview season draws to a conclusion, you will need to rank programs in order of your preference. Once this is done, your list is submitted to the National Residency Matching Program (NRMP) which will match your list against lists from residency programs. Results are released on "Match Day," which marks the official end of your application process. After that, all that's left is signing your residency program contract and graduation.

Comprehensive Timetable

The following is a comprehensive timetable for the application process:

DATES	TASK
3rd year-4th year	Choose a specialty Request letters of recommendation
4th year: July	Request applications from residency programs Register for the Match
July-August	Write curriculum vitae and personal statement Make appointment with Dean for letter
August-October	Mail out completed applications Check on your file with Student Affairs (transcript, Dean's letter, letters of recommendation, and Board scores)
November	Student Affairs mails out your file
October-December	Arrange interviews
November-February	Go on interviews Send thank-you notes within two weeks of interviews
Early February	Complete rank list
Mid March	Match Day
April	Sign and return letters of appointment

This timetable is applicable for students applying for programs that participate in the regular match program. Those applying for specialties that have an early match (ophthalmology, urology, neurosurgery, ear, nose, and throat surgery, and neurology), late match (dermatology), or military match should contact NRMP or the military for specific match details.

THE APPLICATION PROCESS

Letters of Recommendation

Letters of recommendation are an integral component of your application package. Residency programs place a great emphasis on them when considering your candidacy. For this reason, you should start asking for these letters in your third year, after each rotation— whether or not the rotation is in your field of choice. It is better to have too many letters than too few. Most residency programs require that you submit from two to five letters.

Many postgraduate programs expect letters from the faculty of your third-year rotations, as well as letters from any rotations done early in your fourth year. Don't be shy when asking for letters of recommendation, even if you've only worked with the physician for a short period of time. Most doctors expect to be asked, and are happy to write them. Letters must be from attending physicians; they cannot be from residents, interns, or other hospital staff.

Once you have made a career choice, gear your letters toward that field. For example, if you are considering OB-GYN, you should seek at least two letters from physicians in this field with whom you have worked. Additional letters can be from other rotations.

Residency programs place greater value on letters from clinicians who:

- are well known in their field

- know you personally

- think highly of your talents and abilities

- are graduates of the program to which you are applying

Keep in mind that a strong letter from a physician who knows you well is better than a mediocre letter from a nationally-known doctor. Other good sources of letters include your mentor/advisor, research preceptor, or any private physician with whom you have worked closely.

You want to be sure that you get an enthusiastic letter. When you ask for a recommendation, you might say something like, "I would very much appreciate a strong letter of support from you for my residency application. Is that something you would feel comfortable doing?"

Some residency programs require a letter from your school's department chairperson in the field in which you are applying. That person may not necessarily know you. Therefore, you need to make an appointment to see him, so he can spend some time with you in order to get to know you. Based on this encounter (and a review of your files), he will write you a letter of recommendation.

Finally, all postgraduate programs require you to get a Dean's letter. This is not really a letter of recommendation, but a summary of your medical school performance and any other relevant background material. In most schools, the Dean's letter follows a format suggested by the Association of American Medical Colleges. It includes a section for detailing your progress through medical school and your preclinical record with unusually good or poor achievements; a record of your clinical clerkships, focusing on your knowledge, data gathering, analytic reasoning, and interpersonal skills; a report of your special activities, such as research experience, volunteer work, and leadership roles; an analysis of personal qualities which will provide the reader with a sense of who you are as a person (both positive and negative qualities), and a summary recommendation.

Depending on your school, you may or may not have the opportunity to review the Dean's letter once it is completed. If you do see it, be sure all honors, awards, and special activities have been included. Check the letter for accuracy and content before it is sent out, and if there are any discrepancies, bring them to the Dean's attention immediately.

Curriculum Vitae

The CV, a critical component of your application package, is a resume summarizing your skills, accomplishments, and goals. It should be as professional-looking as possible. You are, after all, applying for a job. Make your accomplishments and honors stand out. You can create your own resume on your computer, or have one done for you professionally.

The following are helpful hints for preparing your CV:

- Be concise and to the point. Your CV should be no longer than two pages.

- Emphasize your accomplishments and honors. Bold or underline them for emphasis.

- Design is important. The CV should be easy to read and pleasant to look at.

- Use a reverse chronological approach (most recent to most remote).

- Tailor it to your field of interest.

- Use a laser printer with high quality paper, or have it professionally printed.

Before submitting your CV, have others critique it for content and accuracy, as well as spelling and grammar. Consult your advisors, attendings, other students, or physicians in your specialty. Remember that your CV represents you and is a reflection of your accomplishments; therefore, it is in your best interest to make it as professional and impressive as possible.

Personal Statement

When you first applied to medical school, you were required to write a personal statement. You are now being asked to write one again. Go back to chapter 1 and reread the section on the personal statement; the same rules apply here. Residency programs use this statement to help them assess your personality and to give them insights they cannot get from your transcripts. Once again, this is an opportunity for you to express yourself in a clear, concise statement about who you are, where you come from, and where you are going.

The statement should include your reasons for choosing this particular specialty and your plans for the future. It should emphasize your skills in your area of specialty without bragging or sounding arrogant.

As one doctor who reviews residents' applications told us:

We get a wide variety of personal statements. Some are very straightforward, and some are rather poetic. I do read what they say, but I also look for typographical and grammatical errors. It worries me if an application is sloppy. I want my residents to be rather compulsive; I want them to be people who will be careful and will make sure every detail is correct.

Does that mean that there are people who have not gotten accepted as residents because there were typos on their application? Maybe not. However, there are always some people on the margin. I have to rank my applicants, and the difference between number 20 and number 21 can mean the difference between acceptance and rejection. So it pays to be careful, to proofread it yourself and have others check it over as well.

Completing the Application

Once you have chosen the residency programs that interest you, it is time to request applications. Fortunately, most applications are similar to one another. Some programs even allow you to use a standard NRMP universal application form, which is available through your school. When you receive information or an application from a particular program, the first thing you should do is check its deadline. You don't want to miss being accepted to the program of your choice simply because you were late in filing the papers.

Applications ask standard questions—your name, colleges attended, degrees obtained, research activities, awards, honors, and other relevant information. In addition, some ask questions about your chosen specialty and interest in their programs. They also ask you for the names of physicians who have written you letters of recommendation. Most programs also require a 2" × 2" photograph. The application and photograph get attached to your CV and personal statement.

As you begin requesting residency applications, collecting letters of recommendation, and scheduling interviews, organization becomes more and more important. For each program to which you have applied, you want to keep a record with the following information:

Institution:

Program:

Chairperson:

Address:

Phone number:

Application deadline:

Check when complete:

❑ Application requested

❑ Application received

❑ Application mailed on _____

❑ CV included

❑ Personal statement included

❑ Photo included

- ❏ Program received application
- ❏ Dean's letter mailed
- ❏ Letters of recommendation sent
  1.
  2.
  3.
  4.
  5.

- ❏ Program received recommendations/Dean's letter
  File completed:
  Interview date:
  Thank-you letter sent:

Check off the boxes as items are completed. This way your application status for each program is always up-to-date and readily accessible. Additionally, you can create a file folder for each program, as they will be sending you a lot of information. Be sure to keep written notes about all phone conversations (including the names of the people to whom you speak) and photocopies of all correspondence. Apply early. Interview slots are limited, and may be filled if you wait too long to apply.

Interviewing

Interviews, another critical part of the application process, give the residency program a chance to evaluate the person behind the application. Residency directors are interested in applicants' personalities as well as their skills and accomplishments. Some program directors consider this the most important component of the entire process, so prepare well for your interview. Once again, go back to chapter 1 and reread the section on interviewing. The same principles apply once more.

Interviewing season is usually from October to February. It is a good idea to schedule vacation time or light rotations during this period. The majority of interviews take place in December and January; scheduling your subinternship or a rotation in ICU during this period would be foolhardy. If you are interviewing in several different geographical areas, try to schedule interviews for programs within the same general area during the same time frame so that you can travel easily from one to another.

Before each interview, research the residency program to which you are applying. Go over the information packet you received from the program. Read the brochure and any other material that contains pertinent information. If there are alumni or faculty from that program where you are currently situated, be sure to seek them out for their information and insights.

Although it is impossible to prepare for every question that might be asked, the following are some that are fairly standard:

- Tell me about yourself.

- Why did you choose this specialty?

- Is there any particular medical experience that influenced your choice?

- What was your most interesting case?

- What were your best and worst experiences in medical school?

- If you were the interviewer and had to choose residents for your program, what would you look for?

- Why do you want to do your residency in our program?

- What are you looking for in a residency?

- Where else are you interviewing?

- What rotation did you have the most trouble with?

- Which rotation did you like best or least?

- What types of patients do you have trouble with?

- How do you deal with the competitiveness of some of your colleagues?

- What do you think was missing from your medical education?

- How does your academic record reflect your abilities and potential?

- How do you cope with pressure?

- Was there anything we didn't cover that you'd like to tell me?

You may also be asked questions about current events, clinical scenarios, and your personal and professional philosophies. There are no right or wrong answers. The interviewers are trying to get a sense of who you are and how you handle yourself in a stressful situation.

Successful interviewing is a skill which comes more easily to some people than to others. The key is understanding interviewers' motives. Basically, the interviewer will try to ascertain your:

- interest in the program

- interest in this specialty

- maturity level

- attitude and enthusiasm

- career goals

- performance under stress

- compatibility with the current housestaff

- energy level and intellectual strength

- uniqueness

You will be evaluated through questions and casual conversation. Don't let the seemingly small things trip you up. One residency director told us that he always asks the secretary/coordinator her impressions of the candidates. If they have been rude or uncooperative in setting up the interview session, the candidate comes to the interview with black marks against him. "We had one applicant from Harvard Medical School who looked great on paper. After talking to the coordinator, we discovered he was basically obnoxious—and our interview confirmed her opinion. We didn't want him on our team. After all," says this doctor, "our residents have to work with many people other than their peers. They have to be able to get along with the nurses and the technologists. Their ability to work as part of a team is extremely important."

Go to each interview with a list of prepared questions. Asking thoughtful questions shows interviewers your genuine interest in their program and gives you the opportunity to make sure this is the right program for you.

Here are some sample questions you may want to ask:

- What are the strengths and weaknesses of your program?
- Do you anticipate any major changes in the program?
- Are there research opportunities available?
- What percentages of housestaff successfully match in fellowship positions?
- Where do most of your residents go after graduation?
- Do you help your graduates find jobs?
- Are there any requirements other than clinical responsibilities?
- Are residents allowed to attend conferences?

When deciding if a program is right for you, take into consideration:

- Is the program compatible with your goals?
- Are these people you want to work with?
- Is this an atmosphere you want to work in?
- Does it meet other criteria which are important to you?

The interview will not take up your whole day. Allow time for a tour of the facilities, to meet housestaff, and to attend a conference and/or rounds. This will give you a realistic impression of what the program is like. Ask the housestaff questions on an informal basis. You can often ask them questions you don't necessarily want to pose to your official interviewer. Most will be happy to give you their honest opinion about the program. Questions you may want to ask include:

- Are you happy here?
- What is your opinion of the program?
- What do you like and dislike about the program?
- How is the salary, benefits package, housing, parking, vacations?

- What is the typical patient load?

- How many admissions do you get while on call?

- How often are you on call?

- What are your responsibilities when on call?

- What is the relationship between housestaff and other hospital employees?

- Is moonlighting permitted? Are there opportunities available?

- Is teaching a priority?

- What do you think of the chairperson? Is he or she concerned about the housestaff?

- What made you choose this program?

Be sure to send a thank-you letter to every person who interviewed you within two weeks after your interview. You may also want to send one to the residency director and chairperson. In this letter, you can discuss the things that impressed you most about the program and reiterate your reasons for wanting to be accepted.

Rank Order List

As early February approaches, you should begin to formulate your rank order list. This is a list of all the programs you are considering, from most to least desirable. This may be the most difficult decision you have to make in medical school, so it deserves a lot of thought.

Areas of concern (in no particular order) might include:

- **The overall quality of the program.** Will you be given an appropriate amount of responsibility, or will you have to have approval for every decision you make?

- **Call schedule.** Does this program have a particularly rough call schedule? If so, can you handle it? Do you want to handle it?

- **Location.** You may be at this location anywhere from three to seven years, so you want to be happy there. You may also have a spouse or significant other to consider, as well as your extended family. You might also want to consider the availability of your favorite leisure activities, whether they include skiing, surfing, or going to the museum or theater.

- **Academic strength.** Some programs do more teaching than others. Does the faculty have a strong interest in training residents? This is an important question to ask residents when you visit the program.

- **The atmosphere, ambiance, and personnel.** Does the physical facility make you feel comfortable? Can you see yourself working there for a number of years? What are the people like? Are they friendly? Professional? One of the most important questions to ask yourself is, "Are these the kind of people I'd like to go have a beer with after work?"

- **Reputation.** This is a tricky item. Do you want to attend a program simply because of the prestige factor? If a program with a long-standing reputation matches your needs, of course you should apply. But if it's not really what you want, and if it won't give you the education you really need, you may want to consider other factors first.

Put all your considerations in order of priority. Compare your priorities to each program you are considering. You can then eliminate programs that don't meet your requirements, and rank the ones that are left. Once you have completed this list, you will enter it into the NRMP's computer system. Then you can relax and wait for the results.

The Match Process

Most programs select their residents using the National Resident Matching Process. The purpose of this program is to match each student's highest-ranked program with programs that have offered her a position. The match works in your favor. Residency programs have no information about your rank list. Your decisions are made privately and with no outside pressure. It is to your advantage to fill out your list with the most desirable programs on top. Don't fill out your list based on the order in which you think you'll be selected. You have no way of knowing which programs put you high on their list.

You can rank as many programs as you like. Most students rank several programs in their specialties of choice. They may say, "I want to do medicine at Hospital A, but if I can't do that, I want to do family practice at Hospital B." For example, one medical student's first three choices on his rank order list were:

1. Medicine at Northshore

2. Obstetrics and Gynecology at Long Island Jewish

3. Family practice at Winthrop

Every year, there is a small number of students who do not match. If this should happen to you, don't panic. It doesn't mean that you'll never be accepted into a residency program. There could be many reasons you didn't match and, frankly, you'll never know what they are so it's not worth pondering. You have to take immediate action.

If you don't match, you'll be notified on "Unmatch Day," the day before Match Day. You will also receive a "Result Book," which lists any residencies that have not yet been filled. Starting at 12 noon (EST) on Unmatch Day, you may begin calling any available programs that interest you and try to make a match. You may find programs in your specialty that you did not have on your list. Or you may have to choose another specialty. However, your chances of getting into a program, whether it's in your first choice specialty or not, are good at this point, since these programs need to fill their empty slots.

Fortunately, however, most students will be matched. Remember, your participation in the NRMP is a binding agreement. Wherever you match, you are obligated to attend for at least one year. No exceptions. Therefore, it would be unwise to rank programs which you have no desire to attend.

Come mid-March you will get the results, and shortly thereafter you will receive a contract from the residency program to which you have been accepted. You are then on your way to the next step in fulfilling your dream.

CHAPTER 9

The National Boards

WHAT YOU CAN EXPECT

The first step of the Boards, which you took at the end of your second year, is the best preparation you'll have for the Boards, Step II. Step II, which is given in both September and March of your fourth year, covers material from the clinical years. This exam assesses a student's medical knowledge and understanding of the clinical sciences essential for supervised patient care. Emphasis is placed on health promotion and disease prevention.

USMLE Step II is a two-day, twelve-hour exam. Each day consists of two three-hour sections separated by a lunch break. Like Step I, this is a multiple-choice exam. Questions are either simple-answer (best choice) or extended matching (a long list of answers for a series of questions). Some test questions will be accompanied by pictures, graphs, tables, imaging studies, laboratory data, and other relevant diagnostic studies, which you will be required to interpret and/or identify. Most questions are based on clinical cases for which you will need to provide a diagnosis, a prognosis, an indication of underlying mechanisms of disease, and the next step in medical care or preventive measures.

Topics covered on USMLE Step II include:

- Internal Medicine
- Pediatrics
- Psychiatry
- Obstetrics and Gynecology
- Preventive Medicine and Public Health
- Surgery

Questions are broken down by:

1. Normal conditions
   a. Normal growth and development and general principles of care
   b. Individual organ systems or types of disorders
      1. Infectious and parasitic diseases
      2. Neoplasms
      3. Immunological disorders
      4. Diseases of the blood and blood-forming organs
      5. Mental disorders
      6. Diseases of the nervous system and special senses
      7. Cardiovascular disorders
      8. Diseases of the respiratory system
      9. Nutritional and digestive disorders
      10. Gynecological disorders
      11. Renal, urinary, and male reproductive systems
      12. Disorders of pregnancy, childbirth, and the puerperium (the state of a woman after childbirth)
      13. Disorders of the skin and subcutaneous tissues
      14. Diseases of the musculoskeletal system and connective tissue
      15. Endocrine and metabolic disorders
      16. Conditions originating in the perinatal period
      17. Injury and poisoning

2. Physician tasks
   a. Promoting health and health maintenance
   b. Understanding mechanisms of disease
   c. Establishing a diagnosis
   d. Applying principles of management

3. Population
   a. Age-specific
      1. Prenatal/Perinatal
      2. Infant/Child

3. Adolescent
4. Adult
5. Geriatric
   b. Family and Community
   c. Age-nonspecific

As in Step I, test results are usually mailed to you from six to eight weeks after the exam date and can be interpreted in the same way. After opening the envelope, you will see two numbers. One, a two-digit number, represents a percentile score. The other, a three-digit number, represents a raw score. Raw scores will range between 140 and 260. The mean is 200, and the minimum passing score is 167. This is converted to a two-digit percentile with 82 representing the mean, and 75 representing the minimum passing score. The minimum passing score usually translates to answering between 55 and 65 percent of the questions correctly.

When to Take the Test

It is to your advantage to take the exam as early as possible. The best time to take it is when the course material is relatively fresh in your mind. This means the month of June after your second year for Step I and the month of September at the beginning of your fourth year for Step II. If you take the test early and fail, you have a second chance in the spring. This test has recently become more important as more schools require you to pass Step II before you can graduate. Depending on the school, if you take the exam in March and fail, you may not be able to graduate on time.

Preparation/Study Habits

Obviously, the best preparation technique is consistent studying. That means keeping up with your reading material and making sure you understand concepts as they are presented to you. In actuality, you have been preparing for the Boards since the first day of medical school. In addition, your medical school may have been using Board-type questions on your exams. If you have kept pace with your studies all along, you should be able to pass the Boards with no problem.

If possible, set up your fourth-year schedule so that you have a month off before the exam to review. If this is not possible, try to schedule an easier rotation for the month prior to the exam.

Since you're being tested on a tremendous amount of material, it is (yet again) important to be organized. Some students suggest that you begin reviewing two to three months before the exam. Set up a schedule that allows you to do a reasonable amount of studying but does not interfere with your course load. As the test day approaches, you can increase your review time.

By this time in your medical school career, you have developed your own study style. Stick with whatever works best for you. Some students prefer to reread their textbooks, while others prefer reviewing notes, using review books (see Appendix II), or taking practice exams. Use the combination that makes you feel most comfortable and confident. Keep in mind the amount of available study time and the amount of material you need to cover.

Concentrate on important facts. Don't attempt to memorize material that is totally new to you. Chances are you will forget it before the exam, and if you haven't needed the information by this time, you probably won't need it on the exam. Go over your old course syllabi. Information stressed in your courses is most likely the information that will be stressed on the boards.

Practice exams can help you evaluate your personal strengths and weaknesses. Go back and review areas in which you are weak. Study this material early so that you have time to digest it, and ask others for help if necessary. Take practice exams seriously. Do them under real test conditions. Time yourself. This will help you prepare to sit through the real thing by teaching you to pace yourself. You will have between 40 seconds and one minute to answer each question. This is not a lot of time. Many students have difficulty finishing the exam in time. Time limits are strict, and no exceptions are made. Practice exams will help you increase your speed.

Be sure you are well rested and relaxed the night before the exam. Avoid caffeine or other stimulants. Avoid last minute studying. This will only confuse you and increase your anxiety levels. On the day of the exam, leave yourself plenty of time to get ready and enough time to travel to the test site. Dress comfortably; bring a snack with you, and don't forget your admission ticket and picture ID.

Test-Taking Tips

Your score is based on the number of questions answered correctly. There is no penalty for guessing. If you don't know the answer to a question, take an educated guess. Always try to narrow down your choices by eliminating any answers you know are incorrect. The fewer answers you have to choose from, the better your chances of selecting the right one. Don't change your answers unless you're absolutely sure they're incorrect. Your first instinct is usually your best one.

Use your time wisely. Don't waste it on questions you don't know since all questions carry the same value. Your goal is to answer as many questions correctly as possible. If time permits, you can always go back and review any problems you skipped.

Failure

Inevitably, some students will fail the Boards. This can be traumatic, but it is not the end of the world. Although you will be upset and question your ability to be a doctor, remember that the results are more often an indication of your ability (or inability) to do well on tests.

Learn from your mistakes. On the back of your score sheet you will find a graph showing your overall performance in each subject area. You can determine in which areas you were weak and in which you were strong. Use this information to help you study for your next try.

There are other alternatives, including review courses (either through your school or commercial test preparation services). You may want to review your study habits, and experiment with other, perhaps more effective, methods. Taking the Boards a second time gives you an advantage. You now know exactly what to expect, and have had the opportunity to review areas in which you did poorly the first time. Preparation and commitment will surely lead to success this time around.

Conclusion

Nobody ever said medical school would be easy. It's a long, hard road you've chosen to walk down. And it's just the beginning. Just because you've graduated from medical school doesn't mean you've stopped being a student. Physicians must remain students for the rest of their lives. They learn from studies and scientific data, from textbooks and medical journals, from colleagues and peers, and most of all, from their patients. If you don't have a great love of learning, then medicine is not the right profession for you.

You must also make sacrifices to become a doctor. Your time is not your own. You spend many days and nights away from friends and family. Weekends, holidays, special events—all are meaningless if a patient needs your help.

But this is the choice you've made. For most of you, it was more than a choice—it was a calling. As you face the hardships and difficulties of medical school, there may be times when you question that calling, when your confidence waivers and you give in to your insecurities. You may fear that you can't complete what you have begun. However, remember the words of Babe Ruth, who hit 714 home runs—and struck out 1,330 times:

Never let the fear of striking out get in your way.

Residencies And Fellowships

AEROSPACE MEDICINE

Description: Medical care of individuals involved in aviation and space travel.

Training required: Internship + two years residency

Approximate # of positions available yearly: 77

For information contact:

American Board of Preventive Medicine
9950 W. Lawrence Avenue #106
Schiller Park, IL 60176

or

Aerospace Medical Association
320 S. Henry Street
Alexandria, VA 22314–3579

ALLERGY AND IMMUNOLOGY

Description: Diagnosis and treatment of allergic, asthmatic, and immunological diseases.

Training required: Pediatric or Internal Medicine residency + two-three years training in allergies and immunology

Approximate # of positions available yearly: 175

For information contact:

American Board of Allergy & Immunology
University City Science Center
3624 Market Street
Philadelphia, PA 19104–2675

or

American College of Allergy & Immunology
800 E. Northwest Highway #1080
Palantine, IL 60067

ANESTHESIOLOGY

Description: A hospital-based specialty responsible for giving anesthesia during surgical and other procedures.
Training required: Internship + three years residency
Approximate # of positions available yearly: 1626
For information contact:

American Board of Anesthesiology
100 Constitution Plaza
Hartford, CT 06103

or

American Society of Anesthesiologists
520 N. Northwest Highway
Park Ridge, IL 60068–2573

CARDIOLOGY

Description: Diagnosis and treatment of adult patients with diseases of the heart and circulatory system.
Training required: Three-year fellowship following an Internal Medicine residency
Approximate # of positions available yearly: 926
For information contact:

American Board of Internal Medicine
3624 Market Street
Philadelphia, PA 19104–2675

or

American College of Cardiology
9111 Old Georgetown Road
Bethesda, MD 20814-1699

CHILD AND ADOLESCENT PSYCHIATRY

Description: Diagnosis and treatment of mental, emotional and behavioral disorders in children and adolescents.
Training required: Internship + two years of General Psychiatry residency + two year fellowship in Child and Adolescent Psychiatry
Approximate # of positions available yearly: 400
For information contact:

American Board of Psychiatry & Neurology
500 Lake Cook Road #335
Deerfield, IL 60015

or

American Academy of Child & Adolescent Psychiatry
3615 Wisconsin Avenue N.W.
Washington, DC 20016

CHILD NEUROLOGY

Description: Diagnosis and management of neurological disorders in infants, children, and adolescents.
Training required: Two years of Pediatric residency + fellowship of three years of Child Neurology
Approximate # of positions available yearly: 86
For information contact:

American Board of Psychiatry & Neurology
500 Lake Cook Road #335
Deerfield, IL 60015

or

American Academy of Neurology
2221 University Avenue S.E. #335
Minneapolis, MN 55414

COLON AND RECTAL SURGERY

Description: Diagnosis and surgical treatment of disorders of the intestinal tract, rectum, anal canal, and perianal areas.
Training required: Residency in General Surgery + one year fellowship in Colon and Rectal Surgery
Approximate # of positions available yearly: 50
For information contact:

American Board of Colon & Rectal Surgery
20600 Eureka Road #713
Taylor, MI 48180

or

American Society of Colon & Rectal Surgeons
800 E. Northwest Highway #1080
Palentine, IL 60067

CRITICAL CARE

Description: Managing the overall care of critically ill medical and surgical patients.
Training required: Internal Medicine Residency + one- to three-year Critical Care fellowship
Approximate # of positions available yearly: 117
For information contact:

Society of Critical Care Medicine
8101 E. Kaiser Boulevard
Anaheim, CA 92808–2214

DERMATOLOGY

Description: Diagnosis and treatment of patients with skin disorders.
Training required: Internship + three years residency
Approximate # of positions available yearly: 293
For information contact:

American Board of Dermatology
Henry Ford Hospital
Detroit, MI 48202

or

American Academy of Dermatology
1567 Maple Avenue
Evanston, IL 60201

EMERGENCY MEDICINE

Description: Diagnosis and treatment of acute illness and injury and life-threatening conditions.
Training required: Internship + two or three years residency
Approximate # of positions available yearly: 790
For information contact:

American Board of Emergency Medicine
200 Woodland Pass Suite D
East Lansing, MI 48823

or

American College of Emergency Physicians
P.O. Box 619911
Dallas, TX 75261–9911

ENDOCRINOLOGY, DIABETES, AND METABOLISM

Description: Diagnosis and treatment of patients with diseases of the endocrine (glandular) system and hormonal abnormalities.
Training required: Internal Medicine residency + two- to three-year fellowship
Approximate # of positions available yearly: 266
For information contact:

American Board of Internal Medicine
3624 Market Street
Philadelphia, PA 19104–2675

or

Endocrine Society
9650 Rockville Pike
Bethesda, MD 20014

FAMILY PRACTICE

Description: Responsible for providing primary care for the entire family in office and hospital settings.
Training required: Internship + two years residency
Approximate # of positions available yearly: 2,784
For information contact:

> American Board of Family Practice
> 2228 Young Drive
> Lexington, KY 40505–4294
>
> or
>
> American Academy of Family Physicians
> 8880 Ward Parkway
> Kansas City, MO 64114

GASTROENTEROLOGY

Description: Diagnosis and treatment of patients with diseases of the esophagus, stomach, small and large intestines, liver, pancreas, and gallbladder.
Training required: Internal Medicine residency + two- to three-year fellowship
Approximate # of positions available yearly: 528
For information contact:

> American Board of Internal Medicine
> 3624 Market Street
> Philadelphia, PA 19104–2675
>
> or
>
> American College of Gastroenterology
> 13 Elm Street
> Manchester, MA 01944

GERIATRIC MEDICINE

Description: Primary care and psychosocial problems of older adults.
Training required: Internal Medicine, Family Practice or Psychiatry residency + two- to three-year fellowship

Approximate # of positions available yearly: 150
For information contact:

American Board of Internal Medicine
3624 Market Street
Philadelphia, PA 19104–2675

or

American Geriatrics Society
770 Lexington Avenue #300
New York, NY 10021

HAND SURGERY

Description: Diagnosis and treatment of patients with diseases
of and injuries to the hand and forearm.
Training required: Internship + four years of residency
Approximate # of positions available yearly: 91
For information contact:

American Board of Orthopedic Surgery
400 Silver Cedar Court
Chapel Hill, NC 27514

or

American Academy of Orthopedic Surgeons
22 S. Prospect Avenue
Park Ridge, IL 60068

HEMATOLOGY-ONCOLOGY

Description: Diagnosis and treatment of patients with diseases
of blood (hematology) or cancer (oncology).
Training required: Internal Medicine residency + two-year fel-
lowship
Approximate # of positions available yearly: 400
For information contact:

American Board of Internal Medicine
3624 Market Street
Philadelphia, PA 19104–2675

or

American Society of Clinical Oncology
435 N. Michigan Avenue #1717
Chicago, IL 60611

or

American Society of Hematology
1101 Connecticut Avenue, N.W.
Washington, DC 20036–4303

INFECTIOUS DISEASES
Description: Diagnosis and treatment of patients with contagious diseases.
Training required: Internal Medicine residency + two- to three-year fellowship
Approximate # of positions available yearly: 375
For information contact:

American Board of Internal Medicine
3624 Market Street
Philadelphia, PA 19104–2675

or

Infectious Disease Society of America
201-202 LCI, P.O. Box 3333
New Haven, CT 06510

INTERNAL MEDICINE
Description: Diagnosis and treatment of adult patients with acute and chronic diseases.
Training required: Internship + two years residency
Approximate # of positions available yearly: 266
For information contact:

American Board of Internal Medicine
3624 Market Street
Philadelphia, PA 19104–2675

or

Endocrine Society
9650 Rockville Pike
Bethesda, MD 20014

INTERNAL MEDICINE-PEDIATRICS

Description: Primary care of families without offering obstetric and surgical services.
Training required: Internship + three-year residency
Approximate # of positions available yearly: 315
For information contact:

American Board of Internal Medicine
3624 Market Street
Philadelphia, PA 19104–2675

or

American Board of Pediatrics
111 Silver Cedar Court
Chapel Hill, NC 27514

NEONATAL-PERINATAL MEDICINE

Description: Treatment of babies born prematurely who cannot survive without medical assistance.
Training required: Internal Medicine residency + two- to three-year fellowship
Approximate # of positions available yearly: 285
For information contact:

American Board of Pediatrics
111 Silver Cedar Court
Chapel Hill, NC 27514

or

American Academy of Pediatrics
P.O. Box 927
141 Northwest Point Road
Elk Grove Village, IL 60009–0927

NEPHROLOGY

Description: Diagnosis and treatment of patients with diseases of the kidney and the urinary system.

Training required: Internal Medicine residency + two-year fellowship

Approximate # of positions available yearly: 377

For information contact:

American Board of Internal Medicine
3624 Market Street
Philadelphia, PA 19104–2675

or

American Society of Nephrology
1101 Connecticut Avenue, N.W. #500
Washington, DC 20005

NEUROLOGICAL SURGERY

Description: Diagnosis and treatment of patients with lesions of the brain, spinal cord, peripheral nerves, and their supporting structures.

Training required: Internal Surgery internship + five years residency

Approximate # of positions available yearly: 163

For information contact:

American Board of Neurological Surgery
6550 Fannin Street #2139
Houston, TX 77030

or

American Association of Neurological Surgeons
22 S. Washington Street #100
Park Ridge, IL 60068

NUCLEAR MEDICINE

Description: Diagnosis and treatment of diseases using radioactive materials to image the body's physiological functions.

Training required: Two years of Internal Medicine, Radiology, or Pathology residency + two years of training in Nuclear Medicine
Approximate # of positions available yearly: 144
For information contact:

American Board of Nuclear Medicine
900 Veteran Avenue
Los Angeles, CA 90024

or

American College of Nuclear Medicine
P.O. Box 5887
Columbus, GA 31906

Obstetrics and Gynecology

Description: Obstetricians are responsible for the management of pregnancies and treat disorders of the female reproductive tract. Gynecologists diagnose and treat medical and surgical diseases of the female reproductive tract not involving pregnancy.
Training required: Internship + three years residency
Approximate # of positions available yearly: 1,270
For information contact:

American Board of Obstetrics and Gynecology
936 N. 34th Street #200
Seattle, WA 98103

or

American College of Obstetricians and Gynecologists
600 Maryland Avenue S.W. #300
Washington, DC 20024

Occupational Medicine

Description: Focuses on the effects of specific occupations on health.
Training required: Internship + two or three years residency
Approximate # of positions available yearly: 229

For information contact:

American Board of Preventive Medicine
9950 W. Lawrence Avenue #106
Schiller Park, IL 60176

or

American College of Preventive Medicine
1015 15th Street, N.W.
Washington, DC 20005

OPHTHALMOLOGY

Description: Diagnosis and treatment of patients with diseases and abnormalities of the eye.
Training required: Internship + three years residency
Approximate # of positions available yearly: 525
For information contact:

American Board of Ophthalmology
111 Presidential Boulevard #241
Bala Cynwyd, PA 19004

or

American Academy of Ophthalmology
P.O. Box 7424
655 Beach Street
San Francisco, CA 94120

ORTHOPEDIC SURGERY

Description: Diagnosis and treatment of patients with diseases and injuries of the skeletal system.
Training required: Internship + four years of Orthopedic residency
Approximate # of positions available yearly: 650
For information contact:

American Board of Orthopedic Surgery
400 Silver Cedar Court
Chapel Hill, NC 27514

or

American Academy of Orthopedic Surgeons
222 S. Prospect Avenue
Park Ridge, IL 60068

OTOLARYNGOLOGY

Description: Diagnosis and treatment of patients with surgical problems of the head and neck, the ears, upper respiratory tract, and upper gastrointestinal tract
Training required: One or two years of General Surgery + three to four years of ENT (Ear, Nose, and Throat) training
Approximate # of positions available yearly: 325
For information contact:

American Board of Otolaryngology
5615 Kirby Drive #936
Houston, TX 77005

or

American Academy of Otolaryngology
1 Prince Street
Alexandria, VA 22314

PATHOLOGY

Description: Pathologists study the origin, nature, and course of diseases.
Training required: Internship + four years Pathology residency
Approximate # of positions available yearly: 595
For information contact:

American Board of Pathology
Lincoln Center
5401 W. Kennedy Boulevard
P.O. Box 25915
Tampa, FL 33622–5915

or

College of American Pathologists
325 Waukegan Road
Northfield, IL 60093–2750

PEDIATRICS
Description: Medical care and treatment of children.
Training required: Internship + two-year residency
Approximate # of positions available yearly: 2,411
For information contact:

American Board of Pediatrics
111 Silver Cedar Court
Chapel Hill, NC 27514

or

American Academy of Pediatrics
P.O. Box 927
141 Northwest Point Road
Elk Grove Village, IL 60009–0927

PHYSICAL MEDICINE AND REHABILITATION
Description: Responsible for the care of patients recovering
from accidents or debilitating diseases such as strokes.
Training required: Internship + three years residency
Approximate # of positions available yearly: 283
For information contact:

American Board of Physical Medicine & Rehabilitation
Norwest Center #674
21 First Street S.W.
Rochester, MN 55902

or

American Academy of Physical Medicine
& Rehabilitation
122 S. Michigan Avenue #1300
Chicago, IL 60603–6107

Plastic Surgery

Description: Responsible for the repair or replacement of malformed, injured, or lost organs or tissues.
Training required: General Surgery residency + two- to three-year fellowship
Approximate # of positions available yearly: 210
For information contact:

American Board of Plastic Surgery
1617 John F. Kennedy Boulevard #860
Philadelphia, PA 19103–1847

or

American Society of Plastic
& Reconstructive Surgery
444 E. Algonquin Road
Arlington Heights, IL 60005

Preventive Medicine

Description: Responsible for increasing behaviors to prevent disease and injury, and focus early diagnosis and treatment of disease.
Training required: Internship + two years residency
Approximate # of positions available yearly: 30
For information contact:

American Board of Preventive Medicine
9950 W. Lawrence Avenue #106
Schiller Park, IL 60176

or

American College of Preventive Medicine
1015 15th Street N.E. #403
Washington, DC 20005

Psychiatry

Description: Diagnosis and treatment of patients with disorders of the mind.
Training required: Internship + four years residency
Approximate # of positions available yearly: 1,413

For information contact:

American Board of Psychiatry & Neurology
500 Lake Cook Road #335
Deerfield, IL 60015

or

American Psychiatric Association
1400 K Street, N.W.
Washington, DC 20005

PULMONARY DISEASES

Description: Diagnosis and treatment of patients with diseases of the lungs.
Training required: Internal Medicine residency + two- to three-year fellowship
Approximate # of positions available yearly: 540
For information contact:

American Board of Internal Medicine
3624 Market Street
Philadelphia, PA 19104–2675

or

American College of Chest Physicians
3300 Dundee Road
Northbrook, IL 60062

RADIATION ONCOLOGY

Description: Responsible for the treatment of cancer patients with radiation.
Training required: Internship + three years residency
Approximate # of positions available yearly: 1,027
For information contact:

American Board of Radiology
2301 W. Big Beaver Road #625
Troy, MI 48084

or

American College of Radiology
1891 Preston White Drive
Reston, VA 22091

RHEUMATOLOGY

Description: Diagnosis and treatment of patients with disease of the joints, soft tissues, and blood vessels.
Training required: Internal Medicine residency + two- to three-year fellowship
Approximate # of positions available yearly: 215
For information contact:

American Board of Internal Medicine
3624 Market Street
Philadelphia, PA 19104–2675

or

American College of Rheumatology
60 Executive Park South #150
Atlanta, GA 30329

SURGERY

Description: Diagnosis and treatment of patients with diseases and injuries of the abdomen, breast, and extremities, as well as the care of trauma victims.
Training required: Internship + four years residency
Approximate # of positions available yearly: 2,900
For information contact:

American Board of Surgery
1617 John F. Kennedy Boulevard #860
Philadelphia, PA 19103

or

American College of Surgeons
55 East Erie Street
Chicago, IL 60611

Urology

Description: Diagnosis and treatment of patients with diseases of and injuries to the kidney, bladder, urethra, penis, and testicles.

Training required: Two years of General Surgery residency + three years of Urological Surgery residency

Approximate # of positions available yearly: 250

For information contact:

American Board of Urology
31700 Telegraph Road #150
Birmingham, MI 48010

or

American Urological Association
1120 N. Charles Street
Baltimore, MD 21201–1100

Recommended Textbooks and Review Books

ANATOMY

Anatomy 3rd Edition
Clemente
Williams & Wilkins, 1987
439 pgs.

Atlas of Human Anatomy
Netter
Ciba, 1989
514 pgs.

Clinical Anatomy for Medical Students 5th Edition
Snell
Little Brown, 1995
895 pgs.

Clinical Anatomy Made Ridiculously Simple
Goldberg
Medmaster, 1991
187 pgs.

Clinically Oriented Anatomy 3rd Edition
Moore
Williams & Wilkins, 1992
917 pgs.

Color Atlas of Anatomy 3rd Edition
Rohen, Yokochi
Igaku-Shon, 1993
482 pgs.

Grant's Atlas of Anatomy 9th Edition
Agur
Williams & Wilkins, 1991
650 pgs.

Gross Anatomy–Board Review series 3rd Edition
Chung
Williams & Wilkins, 1995
388 pgs.

NMS Anatomy 2nd Edition
April
Williams & Wilkins, 1990
610 pgs.

Pre-Test Anatomy 7th Edition
April
McGraw Hill, 1993
220 pgs.

Primer of Sectional Anatomy with MRI and CT
Correlates
Barrett, Anderson, Holder, Poliaketi
Williams & Wilkins, 1995
132 pgs.

BEHAVIORAL SCIENCES

Behavioral Science–Board Review Series 2nd Edition
Fadem
Williams & Wilkins, 1994
237 pgs.

Behavioral Science for Medical Students
Sierles
Williams & Wilkins, 1993
539 pgs.

NMS Behavioral Science in Psychiatry 3rd Edition
Wiener, Breslin
Williams & Wilkins, 1995
375 pgs.

Pocket Handbook of Clinical Psychiatry
Kaplan, Sadock
Williams & Wilkins, 1990
335 pgs.

Pre-Test Behavioral Science
Pattishall, Jr.
McGraw Hill, 1993
255 pgs.

Quick Reference to Diagnostic Criteria for DSM IV
American Psychiatric Institute, 1994
358 pgs.

Synopsis of Psychiatry 7th Edition
Kaplan, Sadock
Williams & Wilkins, 1994
1257 pgs.

BIOCHEMISTRY

Biochemistry–Board Review Series
Marks
Williams & Wilkins, 1994
584 pgs.

Clinical Biochemistry Made Ridiculously Simple
Goldberg
Medmaster, 1993
93 pgs.

Essentials of Biochemistry 2nd Edition
Schumm
Little Brown, 1995
382 pgs.

Genetics in Medicine 5th Edition
Thompson, McImes, Willard
Saunders, 1991
500 pgs.

Harper's Biochemistry 23rd Edition
Murray, Granner, Mayck, Rotell
Appleton & Lange, 1993
806 pgs.

Lippincott's Illustrated Review of Biochemistry 2nd
Edition
Champe, Harvey
Lippincott, 1994
443 pgs.

NMS Biochemistry 3rd Edition
Davidson, Sittman
Williams & Wilkins, 1994
584 pgs.

Pre-Test Biochemistry 7th Edition
Chlapowski
McGraw Hill, 1993
210 pgs.

Principles of Biochemistry 2nd Edition
Lehninger, Nelson, Cox
Worth, 1993
1013 pgs.

Principles of Medical Genetics
Gelebiter, Collins
Williams & Wilkins, 1990
340 pgs.

COMMUNITY & PREVENTIVE MEDICINE/ BIOSTATISTICS AND EPIDEMIOLOGY

Appleton & Lange Review of Epidemiology and Biostatistics for USMLE
Hanrahan, Madapu
Appleton & Lange, 1994
109 pgs.

NMS Preventive Medicine and Public Health 2nd Edition
Cassens
Harwal, 1992
497 pgs.

EMBRYOLOGY

Human Embryology 1st Edition
Larson
Churchill, 1993
479 pgs.

Embryology–Board Review series
Fix, Dudek
Williams & Wilkins, 1995

266 Langman's Medical Embryology 7th Edition
Sadler
Williams & Wilkins, 1995

GERIATRICS

Essentials of Clinical Geriatrics 3rd Edition
Kane, Ouslander, Abrass
McGraw Hill, 1994
542 pgs.

NMS Geriatrics Exam Series
Conway, Miller, West
Williams & Wilkins, 1988
111 pgs.

HISTOLOGY

Basic Histology 8th Edition
Junquiera, Carneiro, Kelley
Appleton & Lange, 1995
481 pgs.

Cell Biology and Histology–Board Review series
2nd Edition
Gartner, Hiatt, Strum
Williams & Wilkins, 1993
373 pgs.

Color Atlas of Histology 2nd Edition
Gartner, Hiatt
Williams & Wilkins, 1994
397 pgs.

NMS Histology and Cell Biology
Johnson
Williams & Wilkins, 1991
409 pgs.

Pre-Test Histology and Cell Biology
Klein
McGraw Hill, 1993
248 pgs.

Textbook & Atlas of Histology 3rd Edition
Ross
Williams & Wilkins, 1995
823 pgs.

Wheater's Functional Histology 3rd Edition
Burkitt, Young, Heath
Churchill, 1993
407 pgs.

Internal Medicine

Clinical Radiology–The Essentials
Daffner
Williams & Wilkins, 1993
391 pgs.

Cecil Textbook of Medicine 19th Edition
Wyngaarder, Smith Jr., Bennet
Saunders, 1992
2,380 pgs.

Clinician's Pocket Reference (The Scut Monkey's Handbook)
Gomella
Appleton & Lange, 1993
680 pgs.

Current Medical Diagnosis and Treatment 34th Edition
Schroeder, Tierney, McPhee, Papdakis, Frupp
Appleton & Lange, 1995
1,490 pgs.

Fundamentals of Radiology 4th Edition
Squire, Noveline
Harvard University Press, 1988
355 pgs.

A Guide to Physical Exam and History Taking 6th Edition
Bates
Lippincott, 1995
709 pgs.

Harrison's Companion Handbook 13th Edition
Wilson, etc.
McGraw Hill, 1994
940 pgs.

Harrison's Principles of Internal Medicine
13th Edition
Wilson, Braunwald, Isselbacher, Petersdorf, Martin, Fauci, Root
McGraw Hill, 1994
2496 pgs.

Internal Medicine Pearls
Marsh, Mazzaferri
Hanley & Belfus, 1993
270 pgs.

Medical Secrets "Questions You Will Be Asked"
Sollo
Hanley & Belfus, 1991
568 pgs.

Medicine
Fishman, Hoffman, Klausner, Thaler
Lippincott, 1991
555 pgs.

NMS Medicine 2nd Edition
Myers
Williams & Wilkins, 1994
585 pgs.

Practical Guide to the Care of the Medical Patients 3rd Edition
Ferri
Mosby, 1995
893 pgs.

Pre-Test Medicine 7th Edition
Taragin
McGraw Hill, 1995
260 pgs.

Rapid Interpretation of EKGs
4th Edition
Dubin
Cover Publishers Co., 1989
309 pgs.

Washington Manual of Medical Therapeutics
28th Edition
Ewald, McKenzie
Little Brown, 1995
641 pgs.

MICROBIOLOGY AND IMMUNOLOGY

Clinical Microbiology Made Ridiculously Simple
Gladwin, Tratter
Medmaster, 1993
268 pgs.

Jawetz, Meinich, and Adelberg's Medical Microbiology 20th Edition
Brokes, Batel, Ornston
Appleton & Lange, 1995
652 pgs.

Medical Microbiology Exam and Review
3rd Edition
Levinson, Jawetz
Appleton & Lange, 1994
490 pgs.

Microbiology and Immunology–Board Review series
2nd Edition
Johnson, Ziegler, Fitzgerald, Lukasewycz, Hawley
Williams & Wilkins, 1993
284 pgs.

NMS Immunology 3rd Edition
Hyde
Williams & Wilkins, 1995
316 pgs.

NMS Microbiology 2nd Edition
Kinsbury, Wagner
Williams & Wilkins, 1990
436 pgs.

Pre-Test Microbiology 7th Edition
Titon, Ryan
McGraw Hill, 1993
268 pgs.

Schneierson Atlas–Diagnostic Microbiology
9th Edition
Bottone
Abbot, 1985
89 pgs.

NATIONAL BOARDS, STEP 1

1995 First Aid for the Boards
Bhushan, Le, Amin
Appleton & Lange, 1995
220 pgs.

How to Prepare for Step I Medical Exams
Thornbourgh, Schmidt
McGraw Hill, 1993
216 pgs.

Pass USMLE Step I
Schwenker
Little Brown, 1995
139 pgs.

Review for USMLE Step I
3rd Edition
Lazo, Pitt, Gloriso
Williams & Wilkins, 1994
331 pgs.

Review for USMLE Step I
Barton
Appleton & Lange, 1993
263 pgs.

Rypin's Basic Science Review
16th Edition
Frolich (ed.)
Lippincott, 1993
856 pgs.

NATIONAL BOARDS, STEP 2

Instant Exam Review for USMLE Step II
Goldberg
Appleton & Lange, 1993
363 pgs.

Review for USMLE Step II
NMS Review
Williams & Wilkins, 1994
329 pgs.

Review for USMLE Step II
Catlin
Appleton & Lange, 1993
283 pgs.

Rypin's Clinical Sciences Review
16th Edition
Frolich (ed.)
Lippincott, 1993
431 pgs.

NEUROLOGY

Introduction to Clinical Neurology
Gelb
Butterworth-Heinnemann, 1995
370 pgs.

Neurology–House Officer series
5th Edition
Weiner, Levitt
Williams & Wilkins, 1994
236 pgs.

Neurology Secrets
Rolak
Mosby, 1993
450 pgs.

Pre-Test Neurology
Lechtenberg
McGraw Hill, 1995
236 pgs.

NEUROSCIENCE

Clinical Neuroanatomy for Medical Students
3rd Edition
Snell
Little Brown, 1992
653 pgs.

Clinical Neuroanatomy Made Ridiculously Simple
Goldberg
Medmaster, 1995
90 pgs.

Cranial Nerves
Wilson-Pauwels, Akesson, Stewart
B.C. Decker, 1988
170 pgs.

High-Yield Neuroanatomy
Fix
Williams & Wilkins, 1995
111 pgs.

The Human Brain
3rd Edition
Nolte
Mosby, 1993
466 pgs.

The Human Brain (Study Guide)
3rd Edition
Nolte
Mosby, 1993
173 pgs.

Neuroanatomy
Burt
Saunders, 1993
541 pgs.

Neuroanatomy: An Atlas of Structures, Sections, and Systems 4th Edition
Haines
Williams & Wilkins, 1995
260 pgs.

Neuroanatomy–Board Review series 2nd Edition
Fix
Williams & Wilkins, 1995
416 pgs.

Neuroanatomy Made Easy and Understandable
4th Edition
Liebman
Aspen Press, 1991
148 pgs.

Neuroscience in Medicine
Conn
Lippincott, 1995
650 pgs.

NMS Neuroanatomy
DeMyer
Williams & Wilkins, 1988
388 pgs.

Pre-Test Neuroscience
Siegel
McGraw Hill, 1993
189 pgs.

Principles of Neural Science 3rd Edition
Kandel, Schwartz, Jessel
Appleton & Lange, 1991
1,135 pgs.

Structure of the Human Brain: A Photographic Atlas
Dearmond
Oxford, 1989
202 pgs.

OBSTETRICS & GYNECOLOGY

Appleton & Lange's Review of OB-GYN
5th Edition
Julian, Dumesk, Vontrer
Appleton & Lange, 1995
394 pgs.

Current Obstetrical and Gynecological Diagnosis and Treatment 8th Edition
DeCherney, Pernoll
Appleton & Lange, 1994
1,227 pgs.

Essentials of Obstetrics and Gynecology
2nd Edition
Hacker, Moore
Saunders, 1992
679 pgs.

NMS Obstetrics & Gynecology 3rd Edition
Beck
Harval Publishing, 1993
483 pgs.

OB/GYN for Medical Students
Beckmann, Ling, Baransky, Bates, Herbert, Laube, Smith
Williams & Wilkins, 1992
474 pgs.

OB/GYN Secrets
Federickson, Wilkins-Haug
Hanley & Belfus, 1991
308 pgs.

Pre-Test Obstetrics and Gynecology 7th Edition
Evans
McGraw Hill, 1995
227 pgs.

PATHOLOGY

Basic Histopathology 2nd Edition
Wheater, Burkitt, Stevens, Lowe
Churchill, 1991
232 pgs.

Basic Pathology 5th Edition
Kumar, Cotran, Robbins
Saunders, 1992
772 pgs.

Examination and Board Review Pathology
Newland
Appleton & Lange, 1995
314 pgs.

NMS Pathology 3rd Edition
Livolsi, Merino, Brooks, Saul, Tomaszewski
Williams & Wilkins, 1994
508 pgs.

Pathologic Basis of Disease:
Self Assessment and Review
4th Edition
Comptom
Saunders, 1993
239 pgs.

Pathology–Board Review series
Schneider, Szanto
Williams & Wilkins, 1993
397 pgs.

Pathology Illustrated 4th Edition
Govan, Macfarlane, Callenda
Churchill, 1995
843 pgs.

Pathophysiology and Disease
McPhee, Lingappa, Ganong, Lange
Appleton & Lange, 1995
519 pgs.

Pocket Companion to Robbins 5th Edition
Robbins
Saunders, 1995
617 pgs.

Pre-Test Pathology 7th Edition
Clements
McGraw Hill, 1993
283 pgs.

Robbins Pathological Basis of Disease 5th Edition
Robbins
Saunders, 1994
1,400 pgs.

PEDIATRICS

Appleton & Lange's Review of Pediatrics
5th Edition
Lorin
Appleton & Lange, 1993
222 pgs.

Fundamentals of Pediatrics
Randolph, Kaner
Appleton & Lange, 1994
695 pgs.

The Harriet Lane Handbook: A Manual for Pediatric House Officers 13th Edition
Green (ed.)
Mosby, 1993
658 pgs.

Nelson Essentials of Pediatrics 2nd Edition
Behrman, Vaughan
Saunders, 1994
795 pgs.

Nelson Textbook of Pediatrics 14th Edition
Behramn, Vaughan
Saunders, 1992
1,965 pgs.

Nelson Textbook of Pediatrics (Pocket Companion)
Berhman
Saunders, 1993
538 pgs.

NMS Pediatrics 2nd Edition
Dworkin
Harval Publishing, 1992
550 pgs.

Pediatric Secrets
Polin, Ditmar
Hanley & Belfus, 1989
447 pgs.

Pre-Test Pediatrics 7th Edition
Schaeffer, Kravath, Bennet
McGraw Hill, 1995
250 pgs.

Review of Pediatrics 4th Edition
Krugman
Saunders, 1992
174 pgs.

PHARMACOLOGY

Basic and Clinical Pharmacology 6th Edition
Katzung
Appleton & Lange, 1995
1041 pgs.

Exam & Board Review Pharmacology 4th Edition
Katzung, Trevor
Appleton & Lange, 1995
501 pgs.

Goodman & Gillman's Pharmacological Basis of Therapeutics 8th Edition
Gilman, Rall, Nies, Taglov
McGraw Hill, 1990
1811 pgs.

Lippincott's Illustrated Review of Pharmacology
Harvey, Champe
Lippincott, 1992
459 pgs.

NMS Pharmacology 3rd Edition
Jacob
Williams & Wilkins, 1992
366 pgs.

Pharmacology–Board Review series 2nd Edition
Rosenfeld, Ross, Mitchell
Williams & Wilkins, 1993
357 pgs.

Pre-Test Pharmacology 7th Edition
DiPalma, Barberi, DiGregorio, Ferko
McGraw Hill, 1993
221 pgs.

PHYSICAL AND DIFFERENTIAL DIAGNOSIS/INTRO. TO CLINICAL MEDICINE

Guide to Physical Examination and History Taking
6th Edition
Bates
Lippincott, 1995
709 pgs.

Pocket Guide to Physical Examination and History Taking 2nd Edition
Bates
Lippincott, 1995
238 pgs.

Mosby's Physical Examination Handbook
Seidel, Ball, Dains, Benedit
Mosby, 1995
264 pgs.

NMS Introduction to Clinical Medicine
Lewis, Wilms
Williams & Wilkins, 1991
261 pgs.

Pre-Test Physical Diagnosis 2nd Edition
Cobb, Motycka
McGraw Hill, 1995
175 pgs.

Textbook of Physical Diagnosis
Swartz
Saunders, 1989
646 pgs.

PHYSIOLOGY

Basic Medical Endocrinology 2nd Edition
Goodman
Raven, 1994
332 pgs.

Cardiovascular Physiology 6th Edition
Berne, Levy
Mosby, 1992
298 pgs.

Clinical Physiology Made Ridiculously Simple
Goldberg
Medmaster, 1995
152 pgs.

Color Atlas of Physiology 4th Edition
Despopoulos, Silbernag
Thieme, 1991
369 pgs.

Gastroenterology Physiology 4th Edition
Johnson
Mosby, 1991
176 pgs.

Illustrated Physiology 5th Edition
Mackenna, Callander
Churchill, 1990
325 pgs.

NMS Physiology 3rd Edition
Bullock, Boyle, Wang
Williams & Wilkins, 1995
641 pgs.

Physiology 3rd Edition
Berne, Levy
Mosby, 1992
1071 pgs.

Physiology–Board Review series
Costanzo
Williams & Wilkins, 1995
288 pgs.

Physiology–Essentials of Basic Science
Sperelakis, Banks
Little Brown, 1993
911 pgs.

Pre-Test Physiology 7th Edition
Mulligan
McGraw Hill, 1993
212 pgs.

Renal Physiology 5th Edition
Vander
McGraw Hill, 1995
238 pgs.

Respiratory Physiology 5th Edition
West
Williams & Wilkins, 1995
193 pgs.

Review of Medical Physiology 17th Edition
Ganong
Appleton & Lange, 1995
778 pgs.

Textbook of Medical Physiology 8th Edition
Guyton
Saunders, 1991
1,041 pgs.

PSYCHIATRY

Appleton & Lange Review of Psychiatry 5th Edition
Easson
Appleton & Lange, 1994
178 pgs.

Diagnostic and Statistical Manual of Mental Disorders DSM IV
American Psychiatric Institute, 1994
886 pgs.

NMS Psychiatry 2nd Edition
Scull, Bechtold, Bell, Dubovsky, Neligh, Petersen
Williams & Wilkins, 1990
335 pgs.

Pocket Handbook of Clinical Psychiatry
Kaplan, Sadock
Williams & Wilkins, 1990
335 pgs.

Pre-Test Psychiatry 7th Edition
Woods
McGraw Hill, 1995
213 pgs.

Psychiatry–House Officer series 5th Edition
Tomb
Williams & Wilkins, 1993
292 pgs.

Quick Reference to the Diagnostic Criteria for DSM IV
American Psychiatric Institute, 1994
358 pgs.

Synopsis of Psychiatry 7th Edition
Kaplan, Sadock
Williams & Wilkins, 1994
1257 pgs.

RESIDENCY

Getting Into a Residency–A Guide for Medical Students 3rd Edition
Iserson
Galen Press, 1993
431 pgs.

*Resumes and Personal Statements for Health
Professionals*
Tysinger
Galen Press, 1994

SURGERY

Appleton & Lange Review of Surgery 2nd Edition
Quapnick, Carnerale, Gleidman
Appleton & Lange, 198
156 pgs.

Cope's Early Diagnosis of the Acute Abdomen
18th Edition
Silen
Oxford University Press, 1991
301 pgs.

Current Surgical Diagnosis and Treatment
10th Edition
Way
Appleton & Lange, 1994
1426 pgs.

Essentials of General Surgery
Lawrence
Williams & Wilkins, 1992
403 pgs.

Essentials of Surgical Specialties
Lawrence
Williams & Wilkins, 1993
434 pgs.

NMS Surgery 2nd Edition
Jarrell, Carabasi
Williams & Wilkins, 1991
570 pgs.

Pre-Test Surgery 7th Edition
King, Geller, Chabot
McGraw Hill, 1995
324 pgs.

Principles of Surgery 6th Edition
Schwartz
McGraw Hill, 1994
2074 pgs.

Principles of Surgery (Companion Handbook)
6th Edition
Schwartz
McGraw Hill, 1994
771 pgs.

Principles of Surgery: Pre-Test &
Self-Assessment & Review
Schwartz
McGraw Hill, 1994
228 pgs.

Rush University Review of Surgery 2nd Edition
Economou
Saunders, 1994
563 pgs.

Surgical Secrets 2nd Edition
Abeinathy, Harken
Hanley & Belfus, 1991
331 pgs.

About the Authors

Dr. Mary Ross-Dolen is a clinical fellow in child and adolescent psychiatry at the Columbia-Presbyterian Medical Center/Columbia College of Physicians and Surgeons in New York City. She received her M.D. from the Albert Einstein College of Medicine of Yeshiva University, where she was elected to the Alpha Omega Alpha Honor Medical Society.

Dr. Keith Berkowitz is a resident in internal medicine at North Shore University Hospital. He graduated from New York Medical College.

Dr. Eyad Ali, a graduate of New York Medical College, is a resident in internal medicine at North Shore University Hospital.